MathFlare

Name: ________________________________

Class: ______________

Teacher: ____________________________

<u>Introduction</u>

As parents and educators, we recognize the pivotal role mathematics plays in shaping a child's academic journey and future success. Yet, the path to mathematical proficiency can often seem daunting, fraught with challenges and complexities. That's where the transformative power of MathFlare Workbooks shine through, illuminating the way forward with clarity, precision, and purpose.

Introducing MathFlare Workbooks – a beacon of guidance, a testament to excellence, and a catalyst for achievement. Crafted with meticulous care and expertise, MathFlare Workbooks stand as paragons of educational excellence, designed to nurture young minds, ignite a passion for learning, and develop a deep-rooted understanding of mathematical concepts.

Picture this: your child eagerly delves into the pages of Mathflare Workbook, greeted by a step-by-step guide illuminated with vivid examples that demystify complex mathematical concepts. With each turn of the page, they embark on a journey of discovery, encountering thoughtfully curated practice questions that reinforce learning and hone problem-solving skills. And when they unveil the answers to those very questions, a sense of accomplishment blossoms within them – a tangible reward for their hard work and dedication.

But MathFlare Workbooks are more than just tools for learning; they are pathways to comprehension, fostering a deep-seated understanding of mathematical concepts through a sequential, logical flow. From fundamental principles to advanced problem-solving strategies, every chapter builds upon the last, ensuring a robust foundation upon which future knowledge can be constructed.

As parents, we yearn for nothing more than to see our children thrive, to witness the spark of inspiration ignited within them as they conquer academic challenges with confidence and poise. MathFlare Workbooks serve as partners in this noble endeavor, offering not just practice questions, but the keys to unlocking a world of opportunity.

And for teachers, MathFlare Workbooks stand as invaluable allies in the quest to cultivate mathematical proficiency in the classroom. With answers readily available, instructors can focus on guiding and nurturing their students, confident in the knowledge that MathFlare Workbooks provide a solid framework upon which to build.

In the pages of MathFlare Workbooks, we find not just the promise of academic excellence, but the seeds of a brighter tomorrow. So let us embrace the power of mathematics, let us champion the journey of learning, and let us pave the way for a generation of young minds poised to shape the world. With MathFlare Workbooks as our guide, the possibilities are infinite, and the future, bright.

Table of Contents

Foundations of Arithmetic

Whole Numbers and Operations	1
Fractions Identification	6
Compare the Fractions	10
Equivalent Fractions	13
Fractions Addition: Uncommon Denominator	16
Fractions Subtraction: Uncommon Denominator	19
Fractions Multiplication	22
Fractions Division	25
Mixed Numbers and Improper Fractions	28
Exponents	31
Square and Cube Roots	34
Factors	37
Prime Numbers	42
Greatest Common Factor (GCF)	44
Multiples	50
Lowest Common Multiple (LCM)	55

MathFlare
MATH WORKBOOK
Grade 2
Step by Step Guide and Essential Practice with Answers
Addition Subtraction
Multiplication
Place Value and Expanded Notations
Geometry
MathFlare Publishing

MathFlare
MATH WORKBOOK
Grade 2-3
Step by Step Guide and Essential Practice with Answers
Addition Subtraction
Multiplication and Division
Place Value and Expanded Notations
Geometry
MathFlare Publishing

MathFlare
MATH WORKBOOK
Grade 3
Step by Step Guide and Essential Practice with Answers
Multiplication and Division
Decimals
Place Value and Expanded Notations
Fractions and Geometry

MathFlare
MATH WORKBOOK
Grade 1
Step by Step Guide and Essential Practice with Answers
Counting and Numbers
Addition and Subtraction
Place Value and Expanded Notations
Understanding Time
MathFlare Publishing

MathFlare
MATH WORKBOOK
Grade 1-2
Step by Step Guide and Essential Practice with Answers
Counting and Numbers
Addition and Subtraction
Place Value and Expanded Notations
Understanding Time
MathFlare Publishing

MathFlare
MATH WORKBOOK
Grade 3-4
Step by Step Guide and Essential Practice with Answers
Addition Subtraction
Multiplication Division
Place Value and Expanded Notations
Fractions and Geometry
MathFlare Publishing

MathFlare
MATH WORKBOOK
Grade 4
Step by Step Guide and Essential Practice with Answers
Addition Subtraction
Multiplication Division
Place Value and Expanded Notations
Fractions and Geometry
MathFlare Publishing

MathFlare
MATH WORKBOOK
Grade 4-5
Step by Step Guide and Essential Practice with Answers
Multiplication Division
Place Value and Expanded Notations
Fractions and Geometry
Unit Conversion
MathFlare Publishing

MathFlare
MATH WORKBOOK
Grade 5
Step by Step Guide and Essential Practice with Answers
Multiplication Division
Place Value and Expanded Notations
Fractions and Geometry
Unit Conversion
MathFlare Publishing

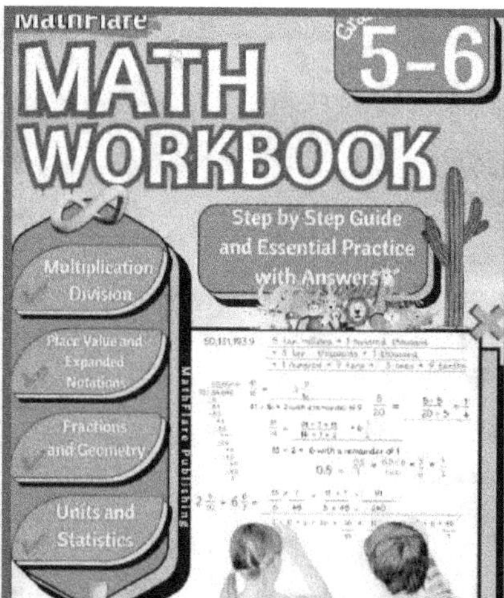
MathFlare
MATH WORKBOOK
Grade 5-6
Step by Step Guide and Essential Practice with Answers
Multiplication Division
Place Value and Expanded Notations
Fractions and Geometry
Units and Statistics
MathFlare Publishing

MathFlare
MATH WORKBOOK
Grade 6
Step by Step Guide and Essential Practice with Answers
Integers and Statistics
Arithmetic and Pre-Algebra
Fractions and Geometry
Ratio and Percentage
MathFlare Publishing

MathFlare
MATH WORKBOOK
Grade 6-7
Step by Step Guide and Essential Practice with Answers
Arithmetic and Pre-Algebra
Ratio, Percent Proportion
Geometry
Statistics
MathFlare Publishing

MathFlare
MATH WORKBOOK
Grade 7
Step by Step Guide and Essential Practice with Answers
Pre-Algebra
Ratio, Percent Proportion
Geometry
Statistics
MathFlare Publishing

MathFlare
MATH WORKBOOK
Grade 7-8
Step by Step Guide and Essential Practice with Answers
Pre-Algebra
Ratio, Percent Proportion
Geometry and Cartesian Plane
Statistics
MathFlare Publishing

MathFlare
MATH WORKBOOK
Grade 8-9
Step by Step Guide and Essential Practice with Answers
Pre-Algebra
Ratio, Proportion and Percentage
Linear Equations
Geometry and Cartesian Plane
MathFlare Publishing

MathFlare
MATH WORKBOOK
Grade 8
Step by Step Guide and Essential Practice with Answers
Pre-Algebra
Percentage
Linear Equations
Geometry
MathFlare Publishing

Operations with Whole Numbers

Positive and negative integers are whole numbers that can represent quantities greater than zero and less than zero, respectively.

Positive Integers: Positive integers are whole numbers greater than zero. They are denoted by the numbers 1,2,3,4...

Negative Integers: Negative integers are whole numbers less than zero. They are denoted by placing a negative sign ("-") before the numbers, such as $-1,-2,-3,-4,...$

The positive integers are used to represent the number of objects, scores, etc. whereas the negative integers can be used to represent debt, losses, temperatures below freezing points, etc.

Let's solve some problems:

1. $6 - (-8) - 9$

- Start by simplifying within the parentheses:

$$-(-8) \text{ becomes } 8.$$

- Rewrite the expression with the simplified part:

$$6 + 8 - 9.$$

- Now perform addition and subtraction from left to right:

$$6 + 8 = 14, \text{ then } 14 - 9 = 5$$

2. $(-5) - (-3) + 10$

$$(-5) + 3 + 10$$

$$(-5) + 3 = -2, \text{ then } -2 + 10 = 8$$

Fractions

Fractions represent parts of a whole. They consist of a numerator (the number on top) and a denominator (the number on the bottom).

For example: we have an orange, and we divide it into 5 equal slices. Each slice represents $\frac{1}{5}$ of the orange. Now, if we take 3 of those slices, we have taken $\frac{3}{5}$ of the orange.

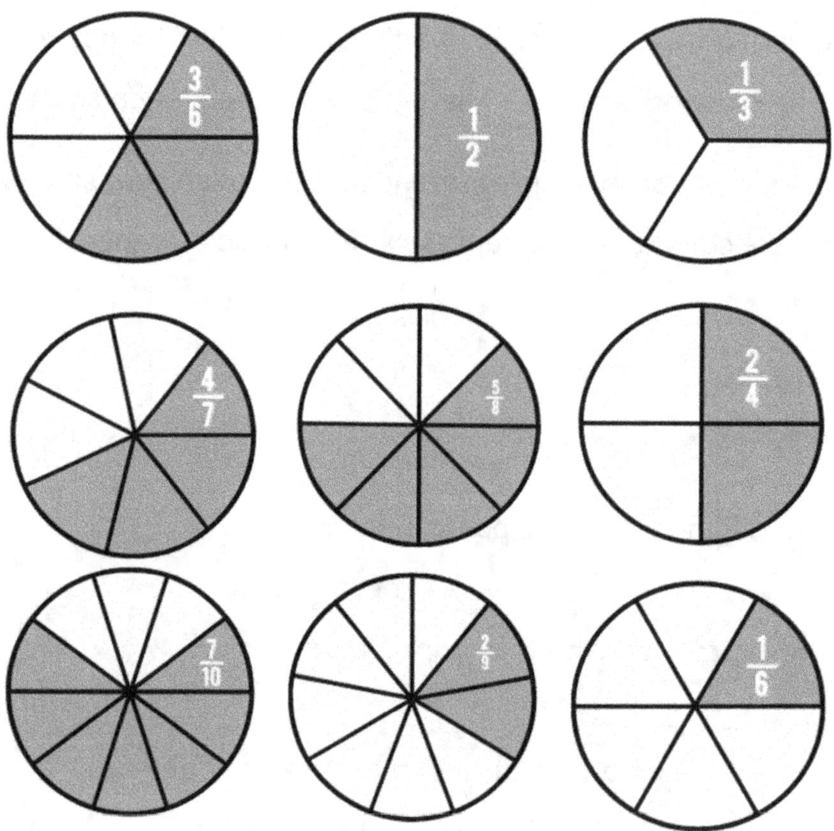

Equivalent Fractions

Equivalent fractions are fractions that represent the same value or part of a whole, even though they may look different.

To find equivalent fractions, you can:

- Multiply or divide both the numerator and denominator by the same nonzero number.
- Simplify fractions to their simplest form.

$\frac{1}{2}$ and $\frac{2}{4}$ are equivalent fractions because if you multiply the numerator and denominator of $\frac{1}{2}$ by 2, you get $\frac{2}{4}$. Similarly, if you divide both the numerator and denominator of $\frac{2}{4}$ by 2, you get $\frac{1}{2}$.

Let's solve a problem:

$$\frac{}{8} = \frac{15}{40}$$

To solve the missing numerator, we can cross multiply.

$$40x = 8 \times 15$$

$$40x = 120$$

$$x = \frac{120}{40} = x = 3$$

$$\frac{3}{8} = \frac{15}{40}$$

Least Common Multiple (LCM)

The Lowest Common Multiple (LCM) of two or more numbers is the smallest multiple that is divisible by each of the numbers.

There are several methods to find the LCM; however, we will focus on only two:

Listing Multiples: List the multiples of each number until you find a common multiple. For example:

$$
\begin{array}{r|l}
8 & 8,\ 16,\ 24,\ 32,\ 40,\ 48,\ 56 \\
\hline
7 & 7,\ 14,\ 21,\ 28,\ 35,\ 42,\ 49,\ 56
\end{array}
\quad , \text{ LCM} = \underline{56}
$$

Division Method: Divide each number with the smallest prime number that divides at least one of the numbers evenly. The product of all the divisors and quotients is the LCM. For example:

$$
\begin{array}{c|cc}
2 & 7 & 8 \\
\hline
2 & 7 & 4 \\
\hline
2 & 7 & 2 \\
\hline
7 & 7 & 1 \\
\hline
 & 1 & 1
\end{array}
$$

$$\text{LCM} = 2 \times 2 \times 2 \times 7 = \underline{56}$$

Both methods have their advantages. For big numbers, using the division way is usually faster. But if we are working with smaller numbers or like seeing patterns, listing multiples might make more sense.

Fractions Addition (Uncommon Denominator)

When adding fractions with uncommon denominators, we need to find a common denominator before we can add them. We will follow the following steps:

1. **Find the Least Common Denominator (LCD).** Determine the least common multiple (LCM) of the denominators.

2. **Convert fractions to have the common denominator** : Rewrite each fraction so that it has the common denominator found in step 1. To do this, multiply the numerator and denominator of each fraction by the same value to make the denominators the same.

3. **Add the fractions:** Once the fractions have the same denominator, add the numerators together and keep the denominator the same.

4. **Simplify, if necessary:** If possible, simplify the resulting fraction by reducing it to its simplest form.

For example, let's add:

$$\frac{5}{11} + \frac{1}{4}$$

The LCM = 2 x 2 x 11 = <u>44</u>

$$\frac{5x4 + 1x11}{11x4} \quad = \quad \frac{20 + 11}{44}$$

$$\frac{31}{44}$$

Fractions Subtraction (Uncommon Denominator)

Fractions subtraction with uncommon denominator follows the same steps except that we subtract instead of adding the fractions.

For example:

$$\frac{5}{11} - \frac{1}{4}$$

$$\text{The LCM} = 2 \times 2 \times 11 = \underline{44}$$

$$\frac{5\times4 \ -1\times11}{11\times4} \ = \ \frac{20 \ - \ 11}{44}$$

$$\frac{9}{44}$$

Fractions Multiplication

To multiply fractions, we simply multiply the numerators together to get the new numerator and multiply the denominators together to get the new denominator.

For example, let's multiply: $\frac{2}{4} \times \frac{1}{4}$

$$\text{Numerator: } 2 \times 1 = 2$$

$$\text{Denominator: } 4 \times 4 = 16$$

$$\text{Therefore, } \frac{2}{16}$$

$$\text{we can simplify the resulting fraction: } \frac{1}{8}$$

Let's solve a problem:

$$\frac{4}{5} \times \frac{4}{5} \ = \ \frac{4 \times 4}{5 \times 5} \ = \ \frac{16}{25}$$

Fractions Division

To divide fractions, we multiply by the reciprocal of the divisor.

For example, let's divide:

$$\frac{6}{8} \div \frac{4}{8}$$

$$\frac{6}{8} \times \frac{8}{4} = \frac{48}{32} = \frac{3}{2}$$

Fractions Addition Word Problems

Aria spent $\frac{1}{3}$ of her salary on watches and then $\frac{1}{2}$ of the money on food. How much money did she spend?

$$\frac{1}{3} + \frac{1}{2} = \frac{2 \times 1 + 3 \times 1}{3 \times 2} = \frac{2 + 3}{6} = \frac{5}{6} \qquad \text{she spent } \frac{5}{6} \text{ of her money}$$

Fractions Subtraction Word Problems

A container has $\frac{2}{5}$ of a gallon of milk. If $\frac{2}{6}$ of the milk is taken out and put into another container, how much milk is left in the original container in gallons?

$$\frac{2}{5} - \frac{2}{6} = \frac{2 \times 6 + 2 \times 5}{5 \times 6} = \frac{12 - 10}{30} = \frac{2}{30} = \frac{1}{15}$$

there is $\frac{1}{15}$ gallons of milk is left in original container.

<u>Mixed Numbers: Mixed into Improper</u>

Mixed numbers and improper fractions are two different ways to represent the same value of a fraction.

1. **Mixed Number:** A mixed number is a combination of a whole number and a proper fraction. For example, $2\frac{1}{3}$ is a mixed number, where 2 is the whole number part and $\frac{1}{3}$ is the fraction part.

2. **Improper Fraction:** An improper fraction is a fraction where the numerator is greater than or equal to the denominator. For example, $\frac{7}{3}$ is an improper fraction because 6 is greater than 3.

To convert a mixed number to an improper fraction, you multiply the whole number by the denominator of the fraction, add the numerator, and then write the result over the original denominator. For example:

$$2\frac{1}{3} = \frac{2 \times 3 + 1}{3} = \frac{7}{3}$$

To convert an improper fraction to a mixed number, we divide the numerator by the denominator. The quotient becomes the whole number part, and the remainder becomes the numerator of the fraction. For example:

$$\frac{7}{3} = 2\frac{1}{3}$$

Let's solve some problems:

$$2\frac{10}{20} = \begin{array}{c} 20 \times 2 = 40 \\ 40 + 10 = 50 \end{array} = \frac{50}{20} = \frac{5}{2}$$

$$\frac{41}{16} = \quad 2\frac{9}{16}$$

$$41 \div 16 = 2 \text{ with a remainder of } 9$$

Factors and Multiples

Factors and multiples are two fundamental concepts in mathematics.

Factors:

- Factors are numbers that divide another number without leaving a remainder.

- For example, the factors of 12 are 1, 2, 3, 4, 6, and 12 because these numbers can divide 12 evenly.

- Factors always come in pairs, except for perfect squares.

Multiples:

- Multiples are the result of multiplying a number by an integer.

- For example, the multiples of 3 are 3, 6, 9, 12, 15, and so on because these numbers are obtained by multiplying 3 by 1, 2, 3, 4, 5, and so on.

- Every number has an infinite number of multiples.

Every factor of a number is a divisor of that number, and every multiple of a number is divisible by that number.

Let's solve some problems:

Factors of **44**

2, 4, 11, 22

Multiples of **77**

77, 154, 231, 308, 385

Least Common Multiple (LCM)

The Lowest Common Multiple (LCM) of two or more numbers is the smallest multiple that is divisible by each of the numbers.

There are several methods to find the LCM; however, we will focus on only two:

Listing Multiples: List the multiples of each number until you find a common multiple. For example:

$$8 \quad \underline{8,\ 16,\ 24,\ 32,\ 40,\ 48,\ 56}$$
$$7 \quad \underline{7,\ 14,\ 21,\ 28,\ 35,\ 42,\ 49,\ 56} \ ,\ \text{LCM} = \underline{56}$$

Division Method: Divide each number with the smallest prime number that divides at least one of the numbers evenly. The product of all the divisors and quotients is the LCM. For example:

2	7	8
2	7	4
2	7	2
7	7	1
	1	1

$$\text{LCM} = 2 \times 2 \times 2 \times 7 = \underline{56}$$

Both methods have their advantages. For big numbers, using the division way is usually faster. But if we are working with smaller numbers or like seeing patterns, listing multiples might make more sense.

Prime Numbers

A prime number is a natural number greater than 1 that has no positive divisors other than 1 and itself.

Rules for Prime Numbers:

1. Prime numbers are greater than 1.

2. Prime numbers have only two distinct positive divisors: 1 and the number itself.

3. Prime numbers are not divisible by any other number except 1 and themselves.

4. 2 is the only even prime number.

Methods for Identifying Prime Numbers:

1. Trial Division: Check divisibility by all numbers up to the square root of the number.

2. Sieve of Eratosthenes: Generate a list of prime numbers up to a certain limit by eliminating multiples of prime numbers.

3. Using Prime Factorization: Factorize the number into its prime factors.

For Example: Let's analyze a few numbers to determine if they are prime or not:

Number	Is Prime?
7	Yes
8	No (divisible by 2)
19	Yes
65	No (divisible by 5)
221	No (divisible by 13)

Greatest Common Factors

The Greatest Common Factor (GCF), also known as the Greatest Common Divisor (GCD), of two or more numbers is the largest number that divides each of the numbers without leaving a remainder. It is the greatest number that is a common factor of the given numbers.

There are two main methods to find the GCF:

- Prime Factorization,
- Using Factors.

Let's find GCF of 44, and 33 using factors:

- List all the factors of each number:

    Factors of 44: 1, 2, 4, 11, 22, 44 Factors of 33: 1, 3, 11, 33

- Identify and chose the common factors:

    The common factor between 44 and 33 is 11.

Exponents and Roots

Exponents

An exponent tells us how many times a number (called the base) is multiplied by itself. It is written as a superscript to the right of the base number. For example, in 2^3, 2 is the base and 3 is the exponent.

Rules:

1. **Product Rule**: When multiplying powers with the same base, add the exponents.

$$a^m \times a^n = a^{m+n}$$

   For example:

$$2^3 = 2 \times 2 \times 2 = 8$$

$$3^2 \times 3^4 = 3^{2+4} = 3^6 = 3 \times 3 \times 3 \times 3 \times 3 \times 3 = 729$$

2. **Quotient Rule**: When dividing powers with the same base, subtract the exponents.

$$a^m \div a^n = a^{m-n}$$

   For example:

$$5^3 \div 5^2 = 5^{3-2} = 5^1 = 5$$

3. **Power of a Power Rule**: When raising a power to another power, multiply the exponents.

$$(a^m)^n = a^{mn}$$

For example:

$$(2^2)^3 = 2^{2\times3} = 2^6 = 64$$

4. **Power of a Product Rule:** When raising a product to a power, distribute the power to each factor.

$$(ab)^n = a^n \times b^n$$

For example:

$$(2\times3)^2 = 2^2 \times 3^2 = 4 \times 9 = 36$$

5. **Power of a Quotient Rule:** When raising a quotient to a power, distribute the power to the numerator and denominator separately.

$$\left(\frac{a}{b}\right)^n = \frac{a^n}{b^n}$$

For example:

$$\left(\frac{4}{2}\right)^3 = \frac{4^3}{2^3} = \frac{64}{8} = 8$$

6. **Zero Exponent Rule:** Any nonzero number raised to the power of zero equals 11.

$$a^0 = 1$$

For example:

$$7^0 = 1$$

7. **Negative Exponent Rule:** A negative exponent means the reciprocal of the base raised to the positive exponent.

$$a^{-n} = \frac{1}{a^n}$$

For example:

$$2^{-3} = \frac{1}{2^3} = \frac{1}{8}$$

To evaluate expressions with exponents, we can use:

- **Repeated Multiplication**: Perform the multiplication indicated by the exponent.

- **Using the Rules of Exponents**: Apply the appropriate rule to simplify expressions involving exponents.

Square Roots

The square root of a number is a value that, when multiplied by itself, gives the original number. It's denoted by the symbol $\sqrt{\ }$.

For example, the square root of 9 is 3 because 3 * 3 = 9.

Cube Roots

The cube root of a number is a value that, when multiplied by itself twice, gives the original number. It's denoted by the symbol $\sqrt[3]{\ }$.

For example, the cube root of 8 is 2 because 2 * 2 * 2 = 8.

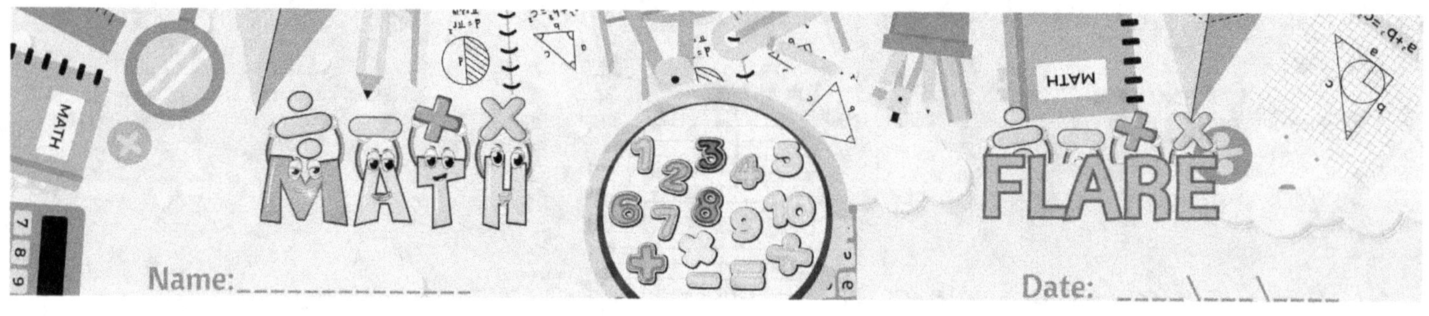

Whole Numbers and Operations

1. $5 + 3 - (8 + 6) =$

2. $(-9) + (-4) + 4 =$

3. $4 - 8 - 7 - 9 =$

4. $7 - (-1) - 2 =$

5. $9 - 2 - 9 =$

6. $1 - (2 + 8) - 5 =$

7. $3 - 10 - 6 =$

8. $4 - 4 - 2 =$

9. $(-7) + (-7) + 7 =$

10. $(-2) + 5 =$

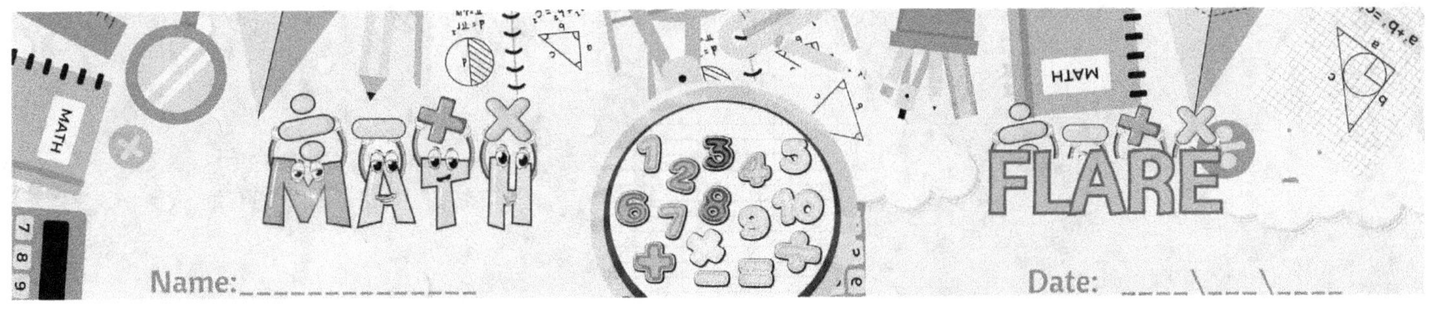

11. $3 + 7 - 5 =$

12. $9 - (2 + 4) + 4 =$

13. $6 + (-2) =$

14. $7 + 8 - 8 =$

15. $10 + (-8) - 8 =$

16. $5 + (2 - 5) =$

17. $4 - (8 + 5) - 10 =$

18. $5 + (2 - 3) =$

19. $3 + (-2) - 6 =$

20. $2 - (7 + 8) + 2 =$

21. $6 + 4 - 4 =$

22. $5 - (7 + 1) - 1 =$

23. $5 - (-8) - 6 =$

24. $6 + (-9) + 6 =$

25. $3 - (7 - 7) =$

26. $(-6) + 8 + (-6) =$

27. $(-2) + (-3) + 5 =$

28. $(-10) + 4 =$

29. $2 - 4 + 6 =$

30. $(-9) + 2 + (-8) =$

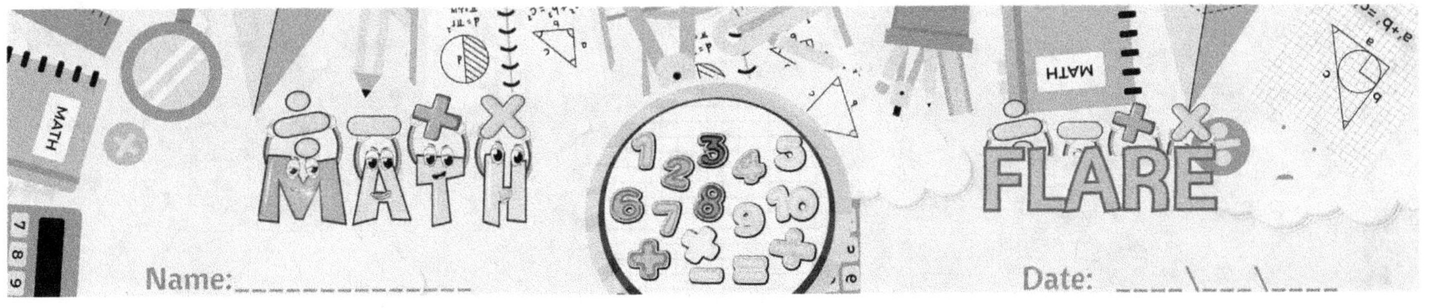

31. $4 + 6 - 9 =$

32. $(-7) + 2 + (-6) =$

33. $(-4) + 3 =$

34. $9 + (-1) - 5 =$

35. $(-10) + 10 =$

36. $10 - 5 - 7 - 7 =$

37. $(-1) + 7 =$

38. $6 - 10 - 5 - 2 =$

39. $6 - 9 + (-2) =$

40. $5 - (1 + 3) + 4 =$

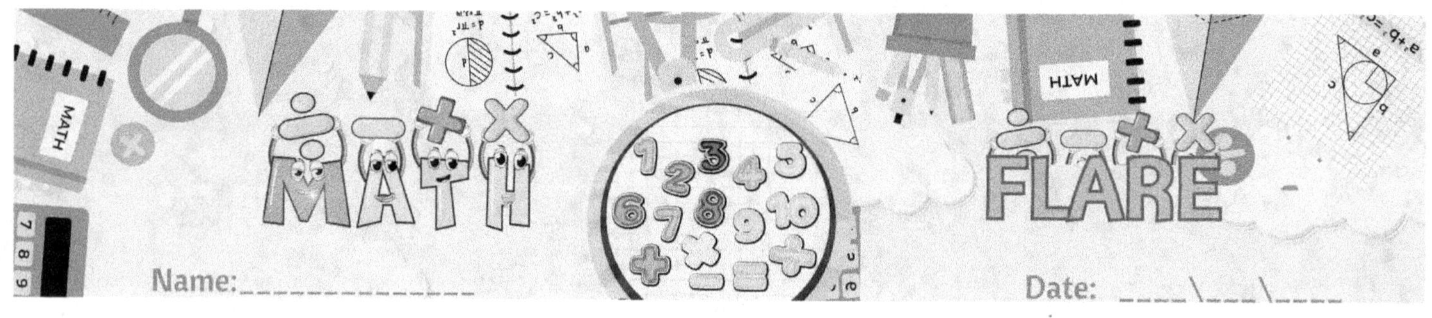

41. $5 - 2 + 3 =$

42. $10 - (3 + 10) - 10 =$

43. $10 - 1 - 2 =$

44. $(-3) + (-3) + 10 =$

45. $5 - 8 - (3 + 5) =$

46. $1 + (-9) + 6 =$

47. $7 - (6 + 3) - 7 =$

48. $8 - 9 - 5 =$

49. $4 - (-8) =$

50. $1 - (1 - 4) =$

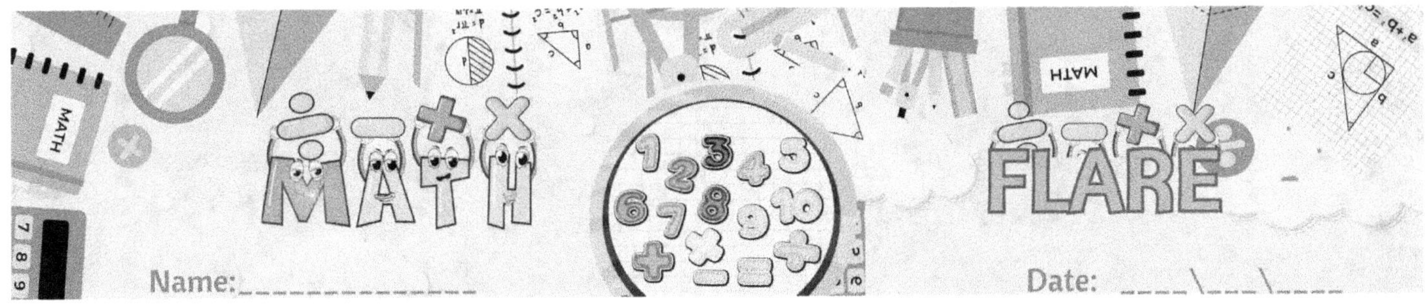

Fraction Identification

Identify fractions of each set of boxes.

51.  =

____

52.  =

____

53. 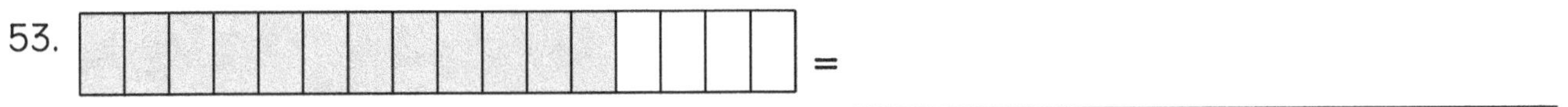 =

____

54.  =

____

55.  =

____

56.  =

____

57. =

____

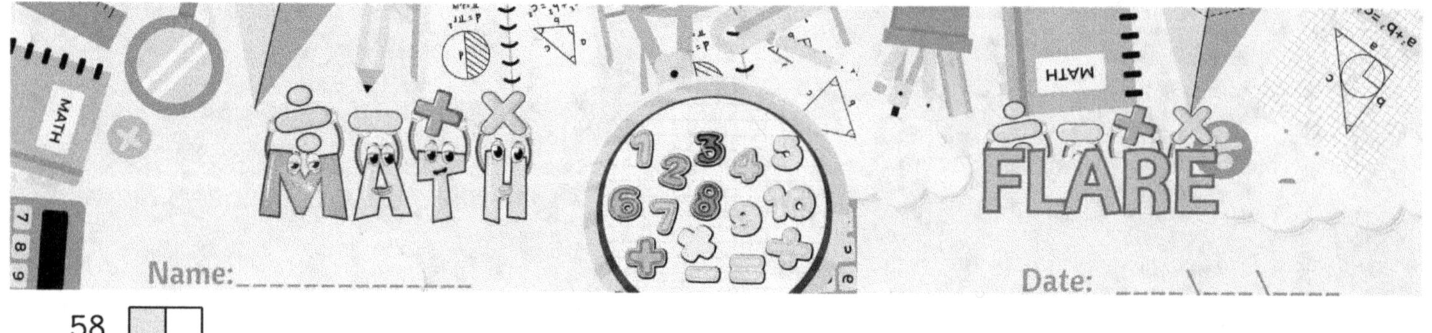

58. 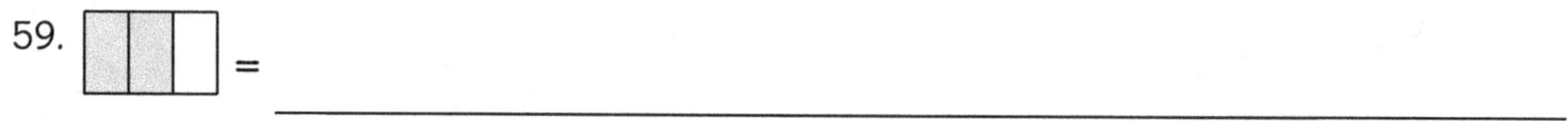 = ____

59. = ____

60. = ____

61. = ____

62. = ____

63. = ____

64. = ____

65. = ____

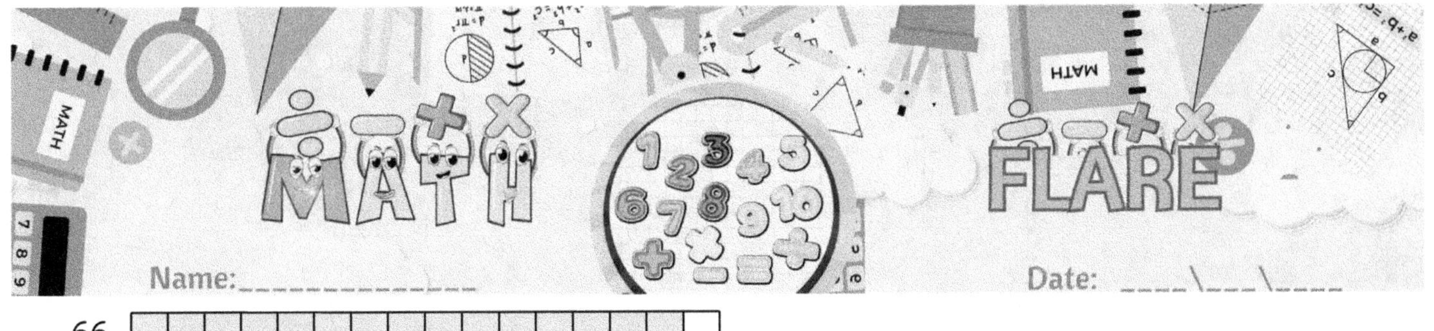

66.  =

67. =

68.  =

69. =

70. =

71. =

72. =

73.  =

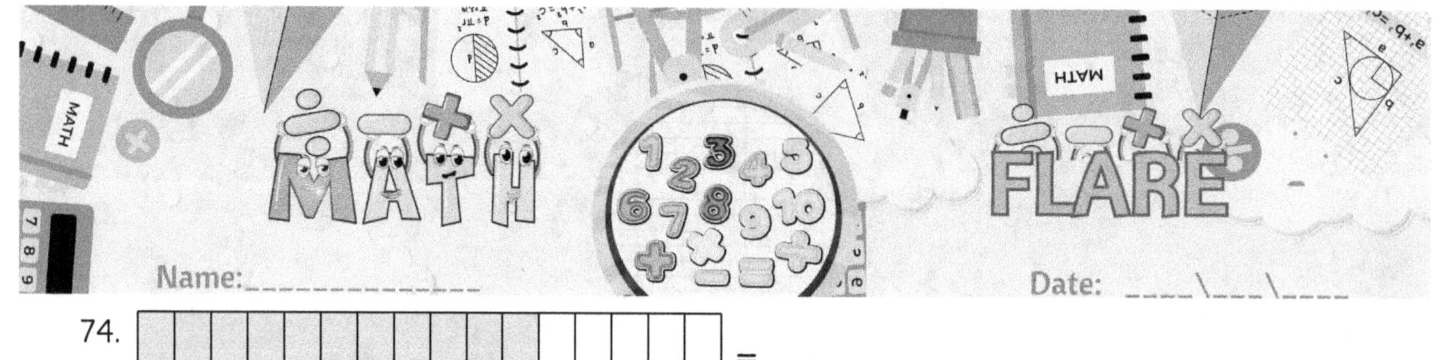

Name:______________________ Date: _______________

74. 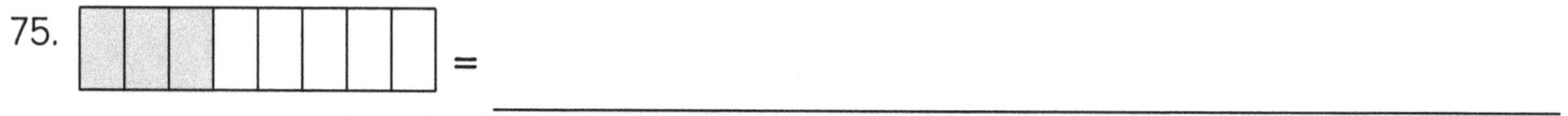 =

____

75. =

____

76. =

____

77. =

____

78. =

____

79. =

____

80. =

____

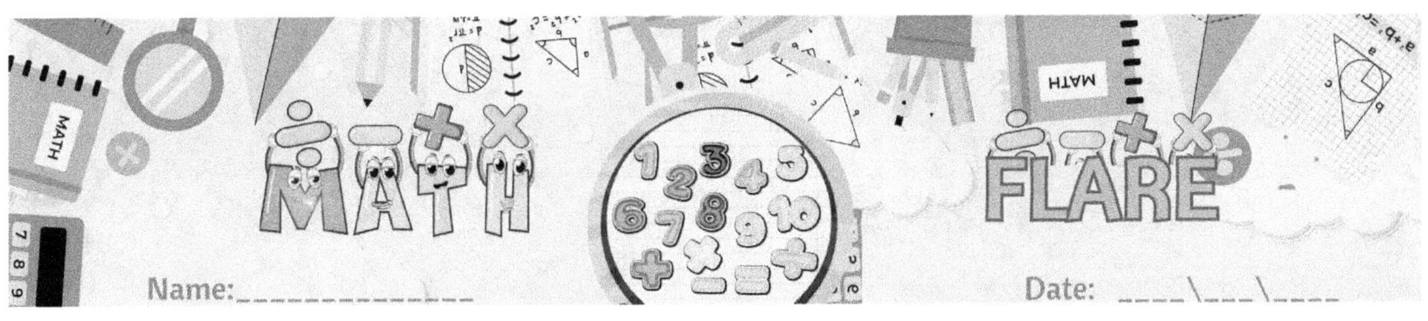

Name:_______________________   Date: ______________

Compare the Fractions

Compare the fractions. Put the signs < , >, or =

81. $\dfrac{1}{19}$ ___ $\dfrac{18}{19}$

82. $\dfrac{3}{18}$ ___ $\dfrac{28}{18}$

83. $\dfrac{6}{12}$ ___ $\dfrac{34}{12}$

84. $\dfrac{4}{8}$ ___ $\dfrac{1}{8}$

85. $\dfrac{4}{10}$ ___ $\dfrac{5}{10}$

86. $\dfrac{26}{14}$ ___ $\dfrac{38}{14}$

87. $\dfrac{35}{18}$ ___ $\dfrac{3}{18}$

88. $\dfrac{2}{7}$ ___ $\dfrac{1}{7}$

89. $\dfrac{14}{11}$ ___ $\dfrac{15}{11}$

90. $\dfrac{6}{17}$ ___ $\dfrac{10}{17}$

91. $\dfrac{85}{105}$ ___ $\dfrac{70}{105}$

92. $\dfrac{16}{13}$ ___ $\dfrac{25}{13}$

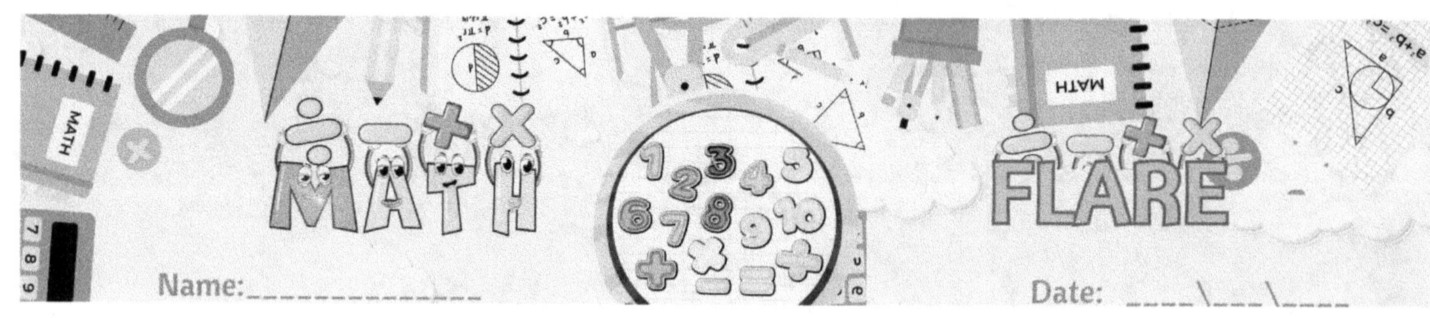

93. $\dfrac{1}{12}$ ___ $\dfrac{5}{12}$

94. $\dfrac{3}{9}$ ___ $\dfrac{26}{9}$

95. $\dfrac{28}{23}$ ___ $\dfrac{21}{23}$

96. $\dfrac{5}{8}$ ___ $\dfrac{2}{8}$

97. $\dfrac{12}{18}$ ___ $\dfrac{20}{18}$

98. $\dfrac{8}{15}$ ___ $\dfrac{38}{15}$

99. $\dfrac{66}{24}$ ___ $\dfrac{43}{24}$

100. $\dfrac{3}{25}$ ___ $\dfrac{7}{25}$

101. $\dfrac{2}{30}$ ___ $\dfrac{7}{30}$

102. $\dfrac{13}{20}$ ___ $\dfrac{6}{20}$

103. $\dfrac{18}{30}$ ___ $\dfrac{15}{30}$

104. $\dfrac{13}{16}$ ___ $\dfrac{37}{16}$

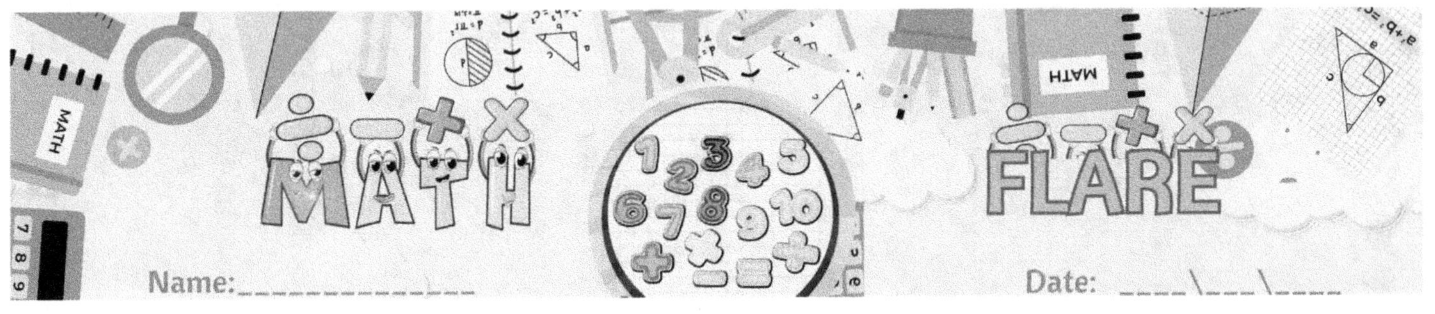

105. $\dfrac{10}{22}$ ___ $\dfrac{32}{22}$

106. $\dfrac{32}{13}$ ___ $\dfrac{34}{13}$

107. $\dfrac{40}{50}$ ___ $\dfrac{26}{50}$

108. $\dfrac{4}{16}$ ___ $\dfrac{5}{16}$

109. $\dfrac{38}{30}$ ___ $\dfrac{9}{30}$

110. $\dfrac{3}{15}$ ___ $\dfrac{1}{15}$

111. $\dfrac{6}{14}$ ___ $\dfrac{16}{14}$

112. $\dfrac{42}{18}$ ___ $\dfrac{3}{18}$

113. $\dfrac{44}{19}$ ___ $\dfrac{41}{19}$

114. $\dfrac{18}{30}$ ___ $\dfrac{6}{30}$

115. $\dfrac{15}{11}$ ___ $\dfrac{25}{11}$

116. $\dfrac{37}{20}$ ___ $\dfrac{2}{20}$

Equivalent Fractions

117. $\dfrac{1}{12} = \dfrac{8}{}$

118. $\dfrac{10}{16} = \dfrac{}{96}$

119. $\dfrac{3}{4} = \dfrac{}{32}$

120. $\dfrac{4}{6} = \dfrac{}{48}$

121. $\dfrac{1}{} = \dfrac{5}{10}$

122. $\dfrac{}{18} = \dfrac{12}{72}$

123. $\dfrac{8}{} = \dfrac{24}{27}$

124. $\dfrac{3}{4} = \dfrac{30}{}$

125. $\dfrac{14}{} = \dfrac{70}{80}$

126. $\dfrac{6}{7} = \dfrac{}{42}$

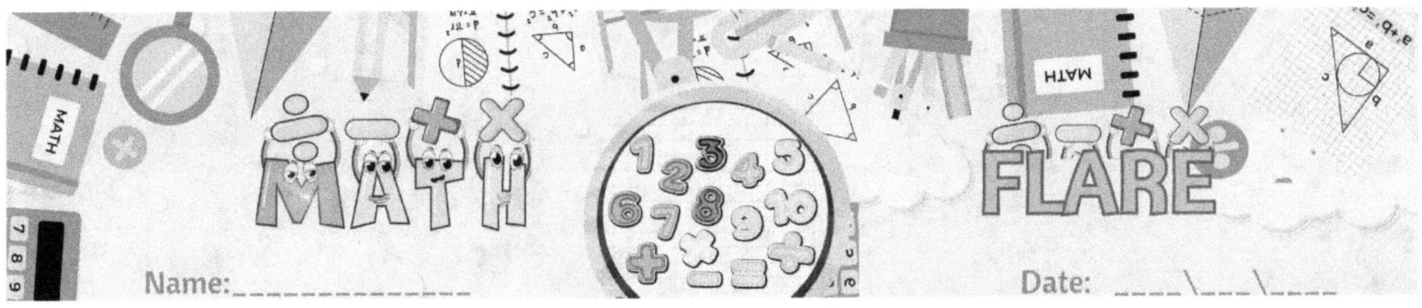

127. $\dfrac{2}{14} = \dfrac{}{140}$

128. $\dfrac{7}{12} = \dfrac{}{24}$

129. $\dfrac{3}{5} = \dfrac{}{20}$

130. $\dfrac{1}{3} = \dfrac{}{18}$

131. $\dfrac{8}{19} = \dfrac{40}{}$

132. $\dfrac{8}{} = \dfrac{64}{80}$

133. $\dfrac{4}{} = \dfrac{32}{120}$

134. $\dfrac{15}{17} = \dfrac{60}{}$

135. $\dfrac{3}{20} = \dfrac{}{200}$

136. $\dfrac{11}{} = \dfrac{66}{78}$

137. $\dfrac{6}{8} = \dfrac{}{48}$

138. $\dfrac{4}{} = \dfrac{28}{77}$

Name:_________________ Date: ______________

139. $\dfrac{}{15} = \dfrac{35}{105}$

140. $\dfrac{1}{2} = \dfrac{8}{}$

141. $\dfrac{}{16} = \dfrac{27}{144}$

142. $\dfrac{5}{17} = \dfrac{10}{}$

143. $\dfrac{7}{} = \dfrac{49}{63}$

144. $\dfrac{2}{} = \dfrac{4}{36}$

145. $\dfrac{17}{19} = \dfrac{51}{}$

146. $\dfrac{1}{} = \dfrac{9}{90}$

147. $\dfrac{6}{} = \dfrac{30}{40}$

148. $\dfrac{2}{} = \dfrac{4}{26}$

149. $\dfrac{3}{11} = \dfrac{}{110}$

150. $\dfrac{4}{} = \dfrac{24}{30}$

Fractions Addition: Uncommon Denominator

Find the sum.

151. $\dfrac{1}{12} + \dfrac{1}{3} =$ _______________

152. $\dfrac{3}{14} + \dfrac{1}{6} =$ _______________

153. $\dfrac{1}{18} + \dfrac{13}{16} =$ _______________

154. $\dfrac{1}{6} + \dfrac{1}{2} =$ _______________

155. $\dfrac{2}{20} + \dfrac{9}{13} =$ _______________

156. $\dfrac{4}{11} + \dfrac{1}{3} =$ _______________

157. $\dfrac{2}{17} + \dfrac{3}{5} =$ _______________

158. $\dfrac{2}{10} + \dfrac{2}{11} =$ _______________

159. $\dfrac{3}{8} + \dfrac{1}{2} =$ _______________

160. $\dfrac{8}{10} + \dfrac{2}{16} =$ _______________

161. $\dfrac{1}{13} + \dfrac{4}{7} =$ _______________

162. $\dfrac{8}{11} + \dfrac{1}{4} =$ _______________

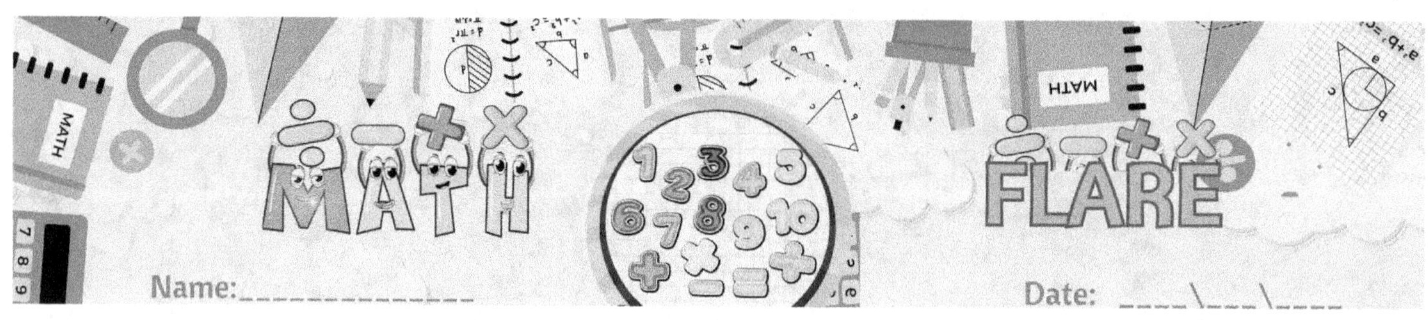

163. $\dfrac{4}{9} + \dfrac{1}{8} =$ _______________

164. $\dfrac{4}{12} + \dfrac{1}{3} =$ _______________

165. $\dfrac{2}{3} + \dfrac{3}{20} =$ _______________

166. $\dfrac{1}{4} + \dfrac{1}{14} =$ _______________

167. $\dfrac{3}{16} + \dfrac{5}{10} =$ _______________

168. $\dfrac{1}{13} + \dfrac{2}{12} =$ _______________

169. $\dfrac{1}{4} + \dfrac{5}{10} =$ _______________

170. $\dfrac{2}{18} + \dfrac{7}{11} =$ _______________

171. $\dfrac{1}{15} + \dfrac{7}{20} =$ _______________

172. $\dfrac{2}{12} + \dfrac{4}{7} =$ _______________

173. $\dfrac{4}{16} + \dfrac{11}{16} =$ _______________

174. $\dfrac{3}{14} + \dfrac{2}{13} =$ _______________

175. $\dfrac{3}{6} + \dfrac{3}{14} =$ _______________

176. $\dfrac{1}{3} + \dfrac{1}{2} =$ _______________

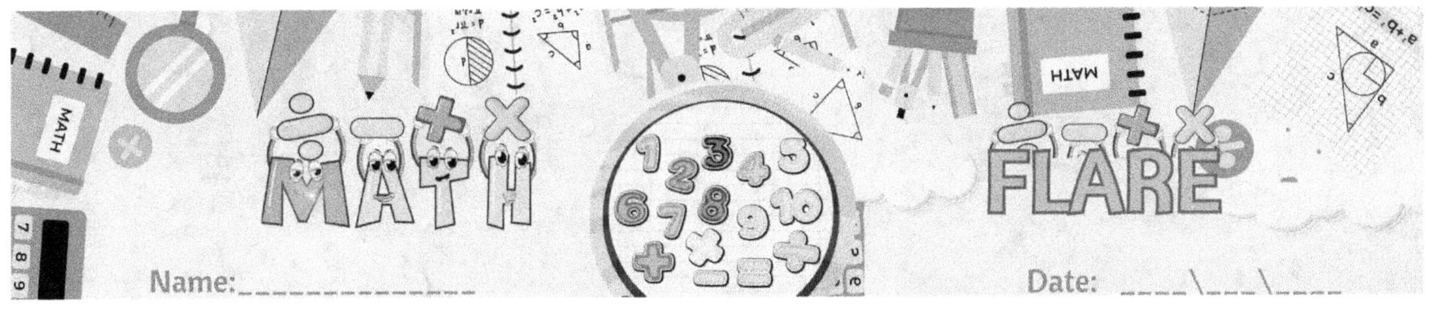

177. $\dfrac{1}{17} + \dfrac{6}{8} =$ _________________

178. $\dfrac{5}{16} + \dfrac{11}{19} =$ _________________

179. $\dfrac{1}{15} + \dfrac{4}{6} =$ _________________

180. $\dfrac{1}{9} + \dfrac{3}{4} =$ _________________

181. $\dfrac{2}{13} + \dfrac{13}{18} =$ _________________

182. $\dfrac{4}{18} + \dfrac{6}{12} =$ _________________

183. $\dfrac{1}{3} + \dfrac{8}{16} =$ _________________

184. $\dfrac{1}{4} + \dfrac{2}{5} =$ _________________

185. $\dfrac{3}{17} + \dfrac{4}{7} =$ _________________

186. $\dfrac{1}{11} + \dfrac{2}{3} =$ _________________

187. $\dfrac{2}{4} + \dfrac{1}{6} =$ _________________

188. $\dfrac{13}{20} + \dfrac{4}{13} =$ _________________

189. $\dfrac{10}{18} + \dfrac{2}{20} =$ _________________

190. $\dfrac{5}{9} + \dfrac{3}{7} =$ _________________

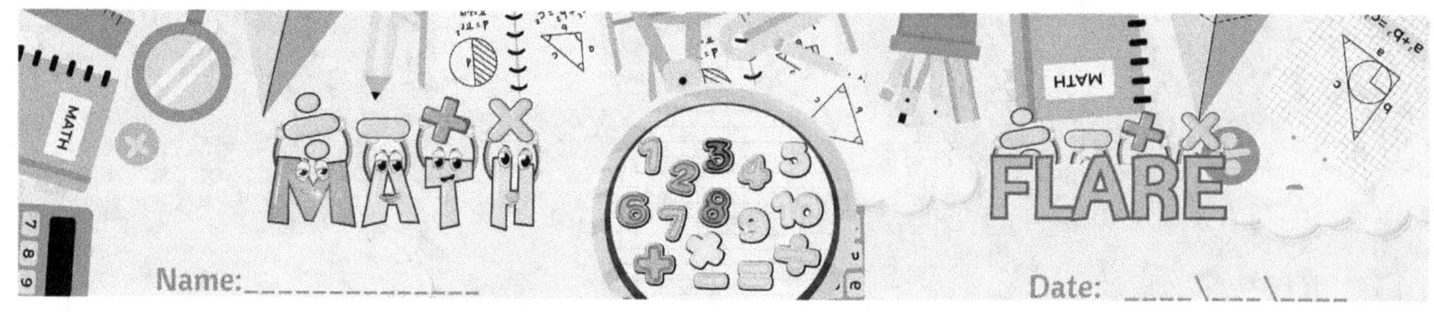

Fractions Subtraction - Uncommon Denominator

Find the difference.

191. $\dfrac{3}{17} - \dfrac{1}{12} =$ _______________

192. $\dfrac{1}{3} - \dfrac{2}{19} =$ _______________

193. $\dfrac{16}{17} - \dfrac{1}{17} =$ _______________

194. $\dfrac{15}{18} - \dfrac{11}{16} =$ _______________

195. $\dfrac{12}{13} - \dfrac{16}{20} =$ _______________

196. $\dfrac{4}{5} - \dfrac{1}{2} =$ _______________

197. $\dfrac{2}{3} - \dfrac{2}{10} =$ _______________

198. $\dfrac{2}{8} - \dfrac{1}{9} =$ _______________

199. $\dfrac{11}{12} - \dfrac{12}{18} =$ _______________

200. $\dfrac{16}{17} - \dfrac{5}{8} =$ _______________

201. $\dfrac{4}{10} - \dfrac{1}{5} =$ _______________

202. $\dfrac{13}{15} - \dfrac{7}{12} =$ _______________

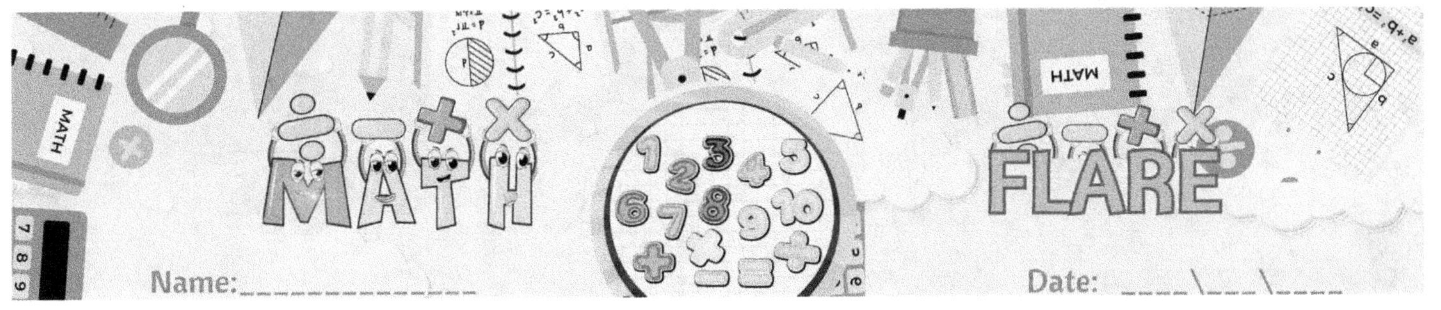

Name:________________ Date: ____________

203. $\dfrac{1}{3} - \dfrac{1}{4} =$ _______________

204. $\dfrac{7}{10} - \dfrac{7}{15} =$ _______________

205. $\dfrac{13}{20} - \dfrac{4}{11} =$ _______________

206. $\dfrac{13}{17} - \dfrac{1}{3} =$ _______________

207. $\dfrac{9}{11} - \dfrac{6}{19} =$ _______________

208. $\dfrac{10}{15} - \dfrac{6}{14} =$ _______________

209. $\dfrac{15}{16} - \dfrac{1}{2} =$ _______________

210. $\dfrac{6}{7} - \dfrac{1}{8} =$ _______________

211. $\dfrac{13}{20} - \dfrac{1}{3} =$ _______________

212. $\dfrac{4}{12} - \dfrac{1}{11} =$ _______________

213. $\dfrac{1}{4} - \dfrac{1}{6} =$ _______________

214. $\dfrac{9}{13} - \dfrac{1}{19} =$ _______________

215. $\dfrac{4}{6} - \dfrac{1}{4} =$ _______________

216. $\dfrac{14}{15} - \dfrac{2}{12} =$ _______________

217. $\dfrac{8}{9} - \dfrac{3}{7} =$ _______________

218. $\dfrac{2}{7} - \dfrac{3}{14} =$ _______________

219. $\dfrac{9}{11} - \dfrac{1}{5} =$ _______________

220. $\dfrac{2}{3} - \dfrac{3}{15} =$ _______________

221. $\dfrac{1}{2} - \dfrac{1}{9} =$ _______________

222. $\dfrac{15}{18} - \dfrac{1}{8} =$ _______________

223. $\dfrac{5}{6} - \dfrac{1}{5} =$ _______________

224. $\dfrac{9}{12} - \dfrac{3}{20} =$ _______________

225. $\dfrac{7}{16} - \dfrac{1}{16} =$ _______________

226. $\dfrac{2}{3} - \dfrac{2}{12} =$ _______________

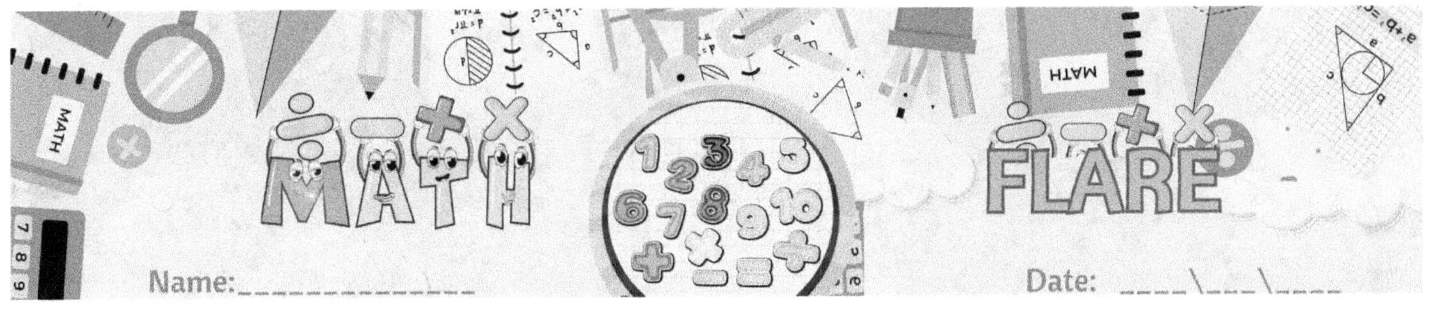

Fractions Multiplication

Find the product.

227. $\dfrac{1}{14} \times \dfrac{1}{13} =$ _______________

228. $\dfrac{2}{5} \times \dfrac{2}{5} =$ _______________

229. $\dfrac{4}{13} \times \dfrac{9}{10} =$ _______________

230. $\dfrac{2}{7} \times \dfrac{11}{15} =$ _______________

231. $\dfrac{1}{3} \times \dfrac{3}{4} =$ _______________

232. $\dfrac{1}{9} \times \dfrac{2}{7} =$ _______________

233. $\dfrac{3}{5} \times \dfrac{1}{2} =$ _______________

234. $\dfrac{3}{8} \times \dfrac{1}{11} =$ _______________

235. $\dfrac{1}{2} \times \dfrac{1}{6} =$ _______________

236. $\dfrac{7}{10} \times \dfrac{1}{5} =$ _______________

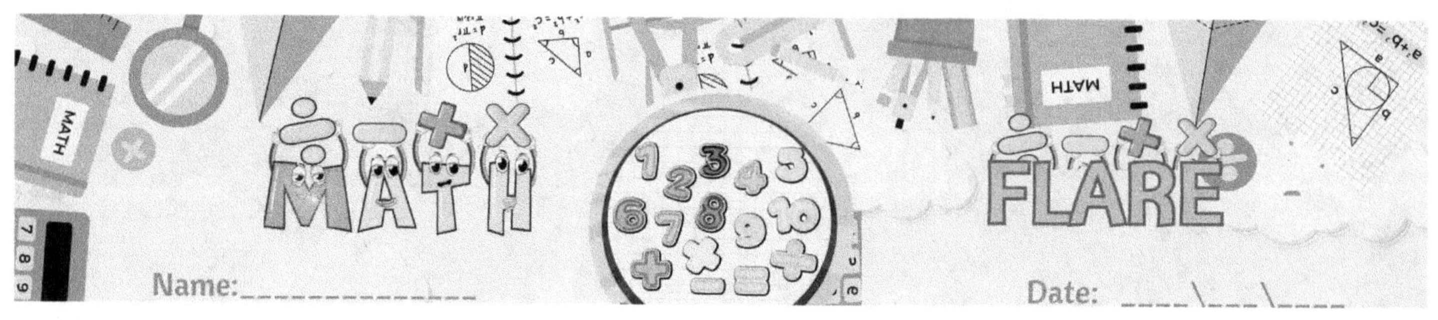

237. $\dfrac{1}{2} \times \dfrac{10}{13} =$ _______________

238. $\dfrac{3}{11} \times \dfrac{1}{5} =$ _______________

239. $\dfrac{2}{3} \times \dfrac{1}{10} =$ _______________

240. $\dfrac{13}{16} \times \dfrac{1}{2} =$ _______________

241. $\dfrac{1}{2} \times \dfrac{3}{8} =$ _______________

242. $\dfrac{3}{8} \times \dfrac{2}{3} =$ _______________

243. $\dfrac{9}{10} \times \dfrac{1}{7} =$ _______________

244. $\dfrac{2}{3} \times \dfrac{1}{3} =$ _______________

245. $\dfrac{2}{3} \times \dfrac{1}{2} =$ _______________

246. $\dfrac{1}{2} \times \dfrac{3}{4} =$ _______________

247. $\dfrac{2}{5} \times \dfrac{3}{7} =$ _______________

248. $\dfrac{7}{11} \times \dfrac{9}{14} =$ _______________

249. $\dfrac{7}{13} \times \dfrac{3}{11} =$ ________________

250. $\dfrac{3}{4} \times \dfrac{4}{5} =$ ________________

251. $\dfrac{4}{9} \times \dfrac{1}{3} =$ ________________

252. $\dfrac{11}{15} \times \dfrac{5}{7} =$ ________________

253. $\dfrac{1}{7} \times \dfrac{1}{2} =$ ________________

254. $\dfrac{5}{13} \times \dfrac{1}{3} =$ ________________

255. $\dfrac{3}{4} \times \dfrac{4}{9} =$ ________________

256. $\dfrac{1}{3} \times \dfrac{5}{8} =$ ________________

257. $\dfrac{1}{3} \times \dfrac{3}{5} =$ ________________

258. $\dfrac{2}{7} \times \dfrac{1}{2} =$ ________________

259. $\dfrac{5}{16} \times \dfrac{1}{6} =$ ________________

260. $\dfrac{7}{10} \times \dfrac{5}{6} =$ ________________

Fractions Division

Find the quotient.

261. $\dfrac{7}{12} \div \dfrac{3}{6} =$ _______________

262. $\dfrac{2}{5} \div \dfrac{5}{8} =$ _______________

263. $\dfrac{1}{6} \div \dfrac{2}{3} =$ _______________

264. $\dfrac{1}{3} \div \dfrac{3}{7} =$ _______________

265. $\dfrac{1}{4} \div \dfrac{1}{11} =$ _______________

266. $\dfrac{3}{10} \div \dfrac{2}{8} =$ _______________

267. $\dfrac{1}{6} \div \dfrac{5}{6} =$ _______________

268. $\dfrac{7}{12} \div \dfrac{4}{5} =$ _______________

269. $\dfrac{1}{2} \div \dfrac{3}{4} =$ _______________

270. $\dfrac{3}{10} \div \dfrac{1}{9} =$ _______________

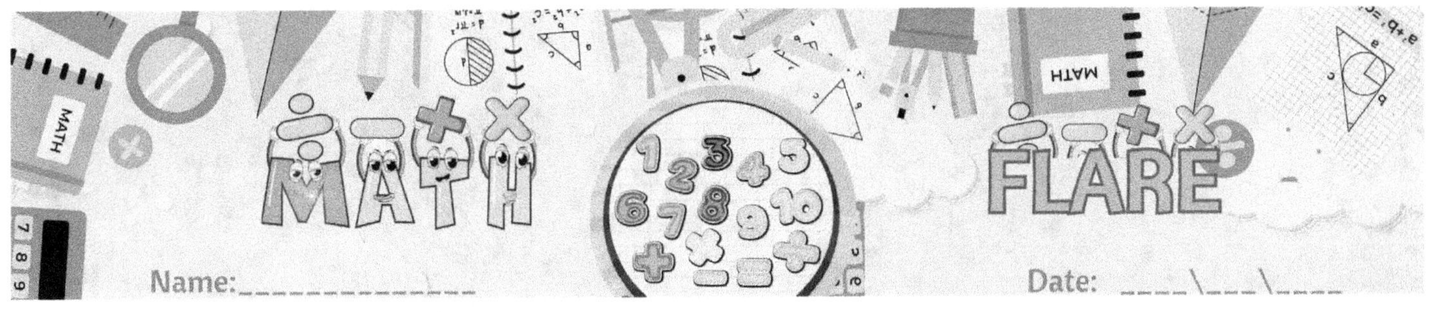

271. $\dfrac{5}{7} \div \dfrac{2}{3} =$ _______________

272. $\dfrac{11}{12} \div \dfrac{1}{8} =$ _______________

273. $\dfrac{4}{5} \div \dfrac{10}{11} =$ _______________

274. $\dfrac{2}{11} \div \dfrac{4}{12} =$ _______________

275. $\dfrac{1}{6} \div \dfrac{1}{2} =$ _______________

276. $\dfrac{1}{2} \div \dfrac{2}{6} =$ _______________

277. $\dfrac{1}{3} \div \dfrac{6}{12} =$ _______________

278. $\dfrac{2}{3} \div \dfrac{1}{2} =$ _______________

279. $\dfrac{1}{5} \div \dfrac{5}{9} =$ _______________

280. $\dfrac{5}{6} \div \dfrac{2}{8} =$ _______________

281. $\dfrac{1}{2} \div \dfrac{8}{11} =$ _______________

282. $\dfrac{3}{11} \div \dfrac{2}{3} =$ _______________

283. $\dfrac{2}{9} \div \dfrac{9}{11} =$ _______________

284. $\dfrac{5}{7} \div \dfrac{4}{6} =$ _______________

285. $\dfrac{2}{3} \div \dfrac{7}{12} =$ _______________

286. $\dfrac{3}{5} \div \dfrac{4}{8} =$ _______________

287. $\dfrac{1}{8} \div \dfrac{1}{5} =$ _______________

288. $\dfrac{1}{2} \div \dfrac{1}{3} =$ _______________

289. $\dfrac{3}{5} \div \dfrac{1}{4} =$ _______________

290. $\dfrac{5}{7} \div \dfrac{1}{10} =$ _______________

291. $\dfrac{1}{3} \div \dfrac{1}{2} =$ _______________

292. $\dfrac{1}{8} \div \dfrac{1}{7} =$ _______________

293. $\dfrac{7}{12} \div \dfrac{1}{2} =$ _______________

294. $\dfrac{10}{11} \div \dfrac{3}{8} =$ _______________

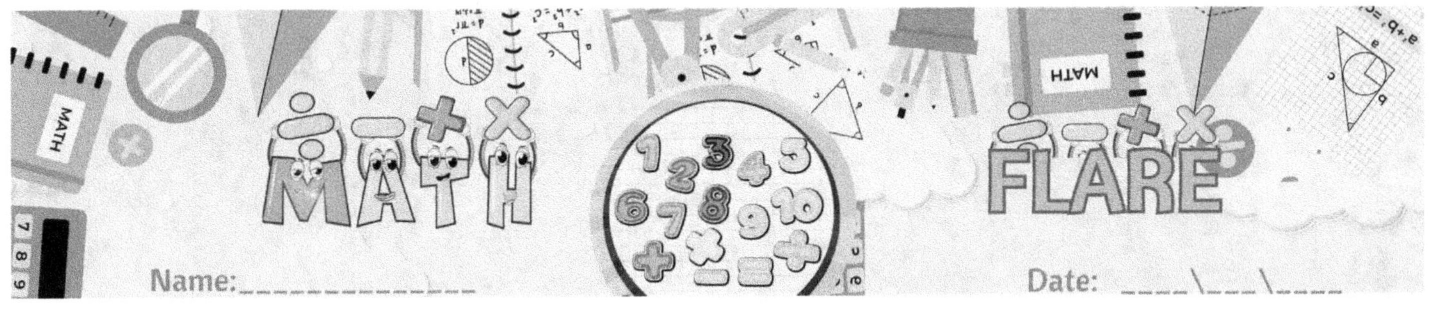

Mixed Numbers: Improper Fractions

295. $8\frac{1}{2} =$ _______________

296. $8\frac{1}{17} =$ _______________

297. $\frac{260}{32} =$ _______________

298. $\frac{47}{12} =$ _______________

299. $8\frac{2}{14} =$ _______________

300. $1\frac{13}{24} =$ _______________

301. $\frac{27}{4} =$ _______________

302. $5\frac{8}{17} =$ _______________

303. $7\frac{17}{28} =$ _______________

304. $3\frac{34}{36} =$ _______________

305. $\frac{87}{10} =$ _______________

306. $8\frac{14}{18} =$ _______________

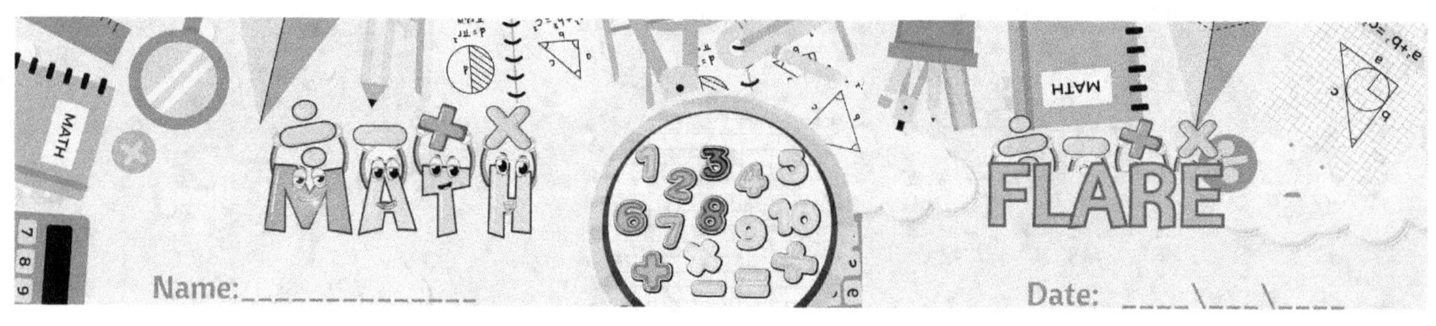

307. $\dfrac{114}{22} =$ ___________

308. $\dfrac{83}{16} =$ ___________

309. $8\dfrac{1}{34} =$ ___________

310. $1\dfrac{11}{32} =$ ___________

311. $\dfrac{37}{5} =$ ___________

312. $7\dfrac{4}{8} =$ ___________

313. $\dfrac{197}{26} =$ ___________

314. $\dfrac{37}{4} =$ ___________

315. $\dfrac{227}{30} =$ ___________

316. $\dfrac{39}{6} =$ ___________

317. $1\dfrac{6}{26} =$ ___________

318. $4\dfrac{5}{9} =$ ___________

319. $7\dfrac{18}{28} =$ ___________

320. $\dfrac{141}{34} =$ ___________

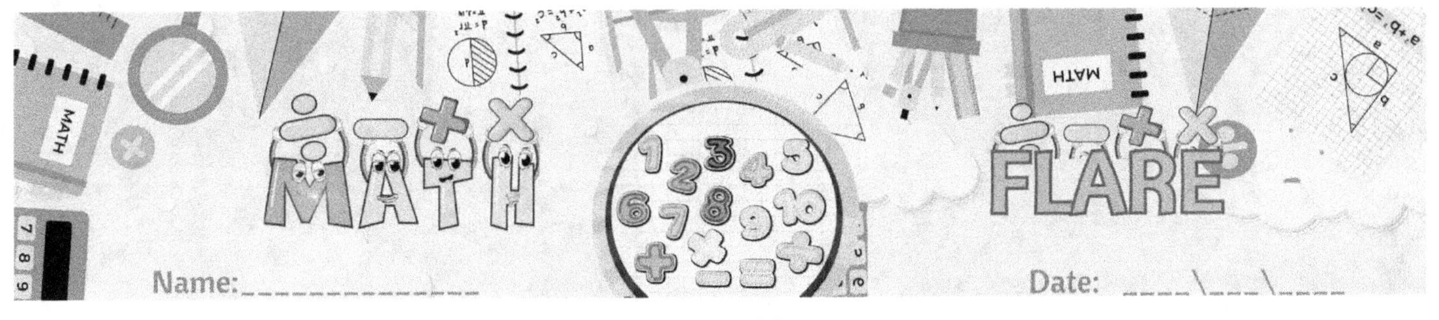

321. $\dfrac{118}{30} =$ _______________

322. $\dfrac{98}{19} =$ _______________

323. $2\dfrac{15}{16} =$ _______________

324. $\dfrac{114}{20} =$ _______________

325. $\dfrac{74}{12} =$ _______________

326. $2\dfrac{13}{16} =$ _______________

327. $\dfrac{9}{5} =$ _______________

328. $\dfrac{74}{9} =$ _______________

329. $9\dfrac{18}{19} =$ _______________

330. $8\dfrac{2}{8} =$ _______________

331. $7\dfrac{2}{15} =$ _______________

332. $\dfrac{7}{2} =$ _______________

333. $\dfrac{32}{14} =$ _______________

334. $\dfrac{80}{11} =$ _______________

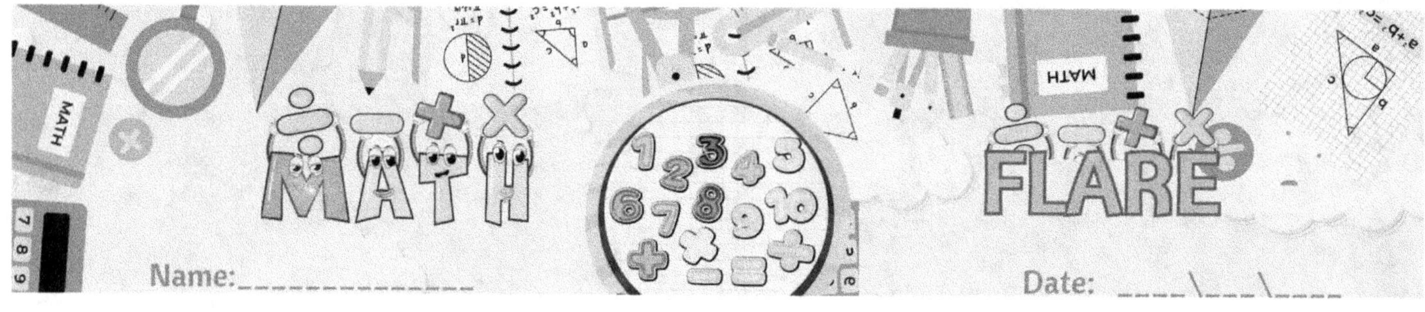

Exponents

Convert the values.

335. 12^{3} =

336. 20^{4} =

337. 1^{2} =

338. 18^{-3} =

339. 15^{4} =

340. 10^{-3} =

341. 20^{3} =

342. 17^{4} =

343. 13^{-3} =

344. 1^{-2} =

345. 14^{-2} =

346. 18^{-2} =

347. 8^{2} =

348. 8^{3} =

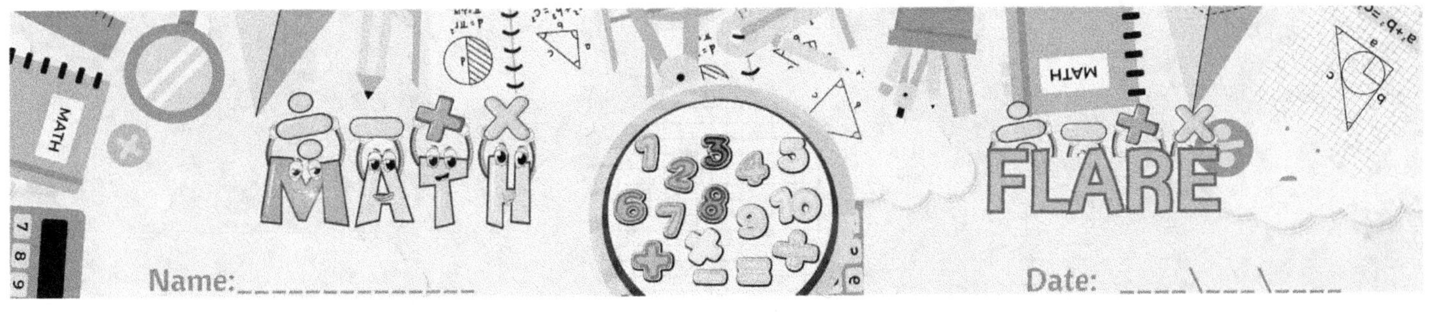

349. $5^4 =$ _______________

350. $4^{-2} =$ _______________

351. $13^2 =$ _______________

352. $4^2 =$ _______________

353. $11^{-3} =$ _______________

354. $19^{-3} =$ _______________

355. $4^3 =$ _______________

356. $9^3 =$ _______________

357. $17^2 =$ _______________

358. $4^4 =$ _______________

359. $11^{-2} =$ _______________

360. $15^{-3} =$ _______________

361. $15^{-2} =$ _______________

362. $19^{-2} =$ _______________

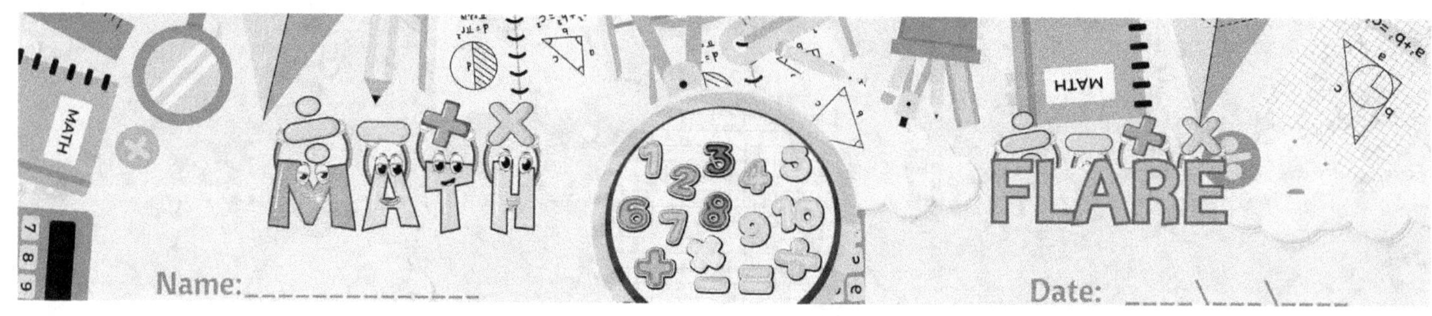

363. $13^4 =$ _______________

364. $12^{-2} =$ _______________

365. $1^{-3} =$ _______________

366. $3^{-3} =$ _______________

367. $6^{-3} =$ _______________

368. $6^{-2} =$ _______________

369. $11^2 =$ _______________

370. $2^{-2} =$ _______________

371. $16^2 =$ _______________

372. $5^{-2} =$ _______________

373. $2^3 =$ _______________

374. $9^2 =$ _______________

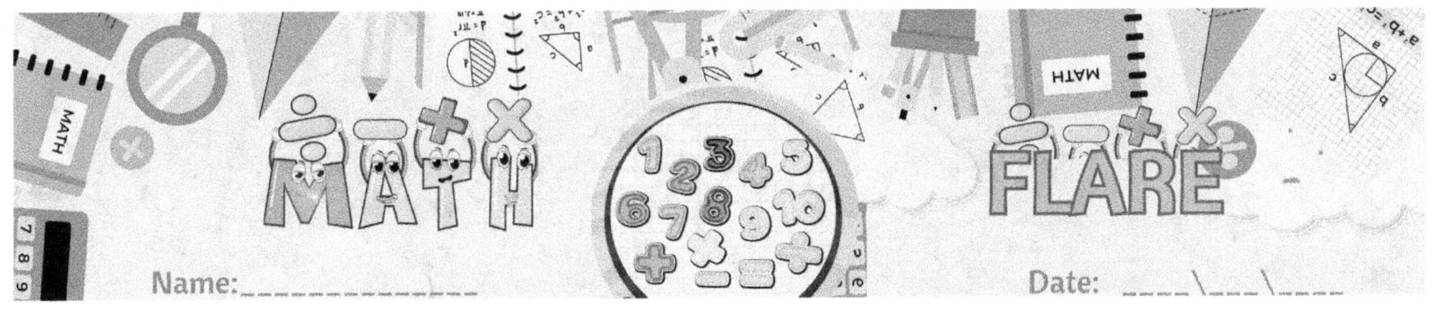

Square and Cube Roots

Calculate the root of each value.

375. $\sqrt[3]{1}$ = _______________

376. $\sqrt[3]{125}$ = _______________

377. $\sqrt[4]{625}$ = _______________

378. $\sqrt[4]{16}$ = _______________

379. $\sqrt[3]{512}$ = _______________

380. $\sqrt[3]{5,832}$ = _______________

381. $\sqrt[4]{1,296}$ = _______________

382. $\sqrt{361}$ = _______________

383. $\sqrt[3]{8}$ = _______________

384. $\sqrt[4]{81}$ = _______________

385. $\sqrt{1,764}$ = _______________

386. $\sqrt[3]{9,261}$ = _______________

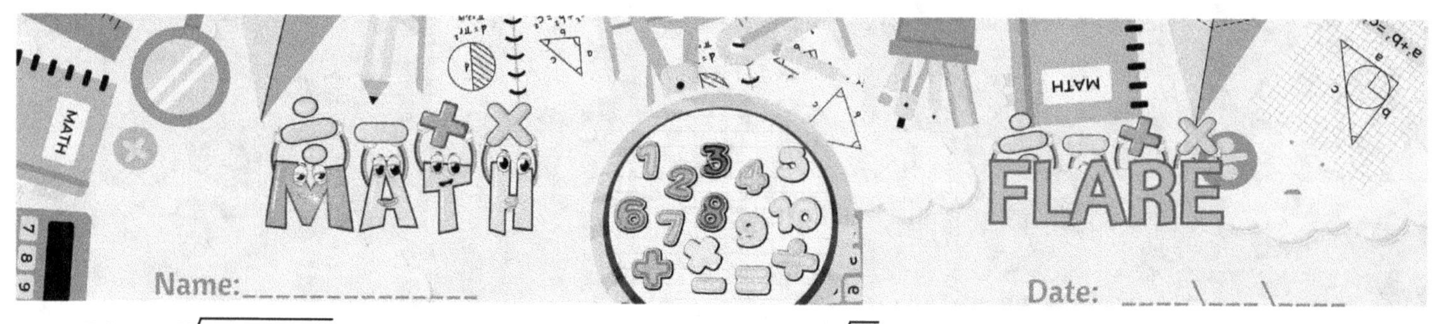

387. $\sqrt[3]{10,648}$ = _____________

388. $\sqrt[4]{1}$ = _____________

389. $\sqrt[4]{6,561}$ = _____________

390. $\sqrt[3]{4,913}$ = _____________

391. $\sqrt{324}$ = _____________

392. $\sqrt[3]{64}$ = _____________

393. $\sqrt{144}$ = _____________

394. $\sqrt{2,601}$ = _____________

395. $\sqrt[3]{27}$ = _____________

396. $\sqrt{9,604}$ = _____________

397. $\sqrt[3]{3,375}$ = _____________

398. $\sqrt{9}$ = _____________

399. $\sqrt[4]{4,096}$ = _____________

400. $\sqrt[3]{343}$ = _____________

401. $\sqrt[4]{10,000}$ = _____________

402. $\sqrt{100}$ = _____________

403. $\sqrt{64}$ = _____________

404. $\sqrt{289}$ = _____________

405. $\sqrt{529}$ = _____________

406. $\sqrt[3]{2,197}$ = _____________

407. $\sqrt{576}$ = _____________

408. $\sqrt{25}$ = _____________

409. $\sqrt{169}$ = _____________

410. $\sqrt{729}$ = _____________

411. $\sqrt[3]{8,000}$ = _____________

412. $\sqrt{81}$ = _____________

413. $\sqrt[3]{216}$ = _____________

414. $\sqrt{49}$ = _____________

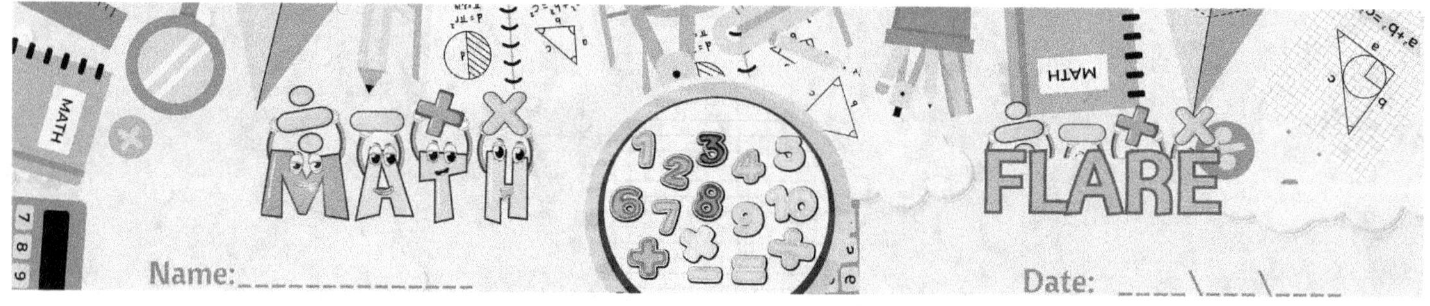

Factors

415. 1 _______________________________________

416. 18 _______________________________________

417. 395 _______________________________________

418. 98 _______________________________________

419. 7 _______________________________________

420. 2 _______________________________________

421. 23 _______________________________________

422. 11 _______________________________________

423. 43 _______________________________

424. 70 _______________________________

425. 8 _______________________________

426. 387 _______________________________

427. 464 _______________________________

428. 76 _______________________________

429. 75 _______________________________

430. 24 _______________________________

431. 5

432. 87

433. 115

434. 65

435. 68

436. 62

437. 6

438. 9

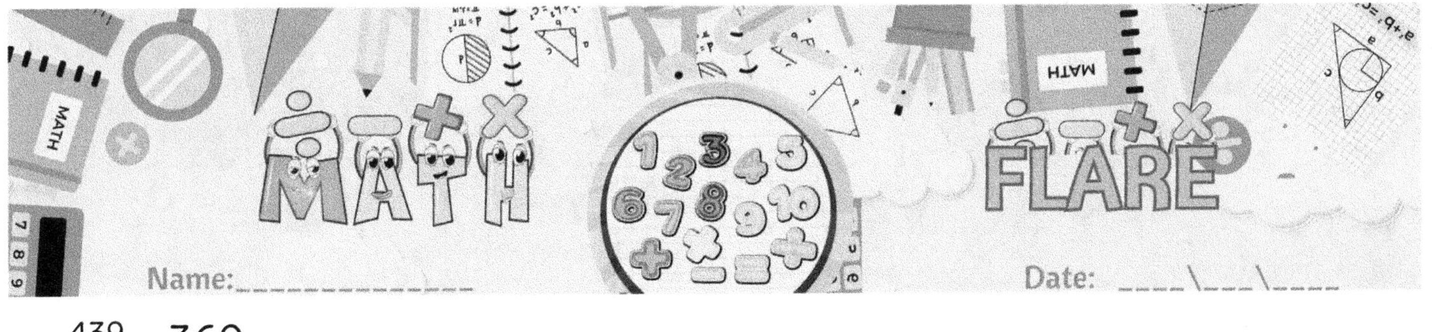

439. 360 ____

440. 336 ____

441. 59 ____

442. 49 ____

443. 128 ____

444. 61 ____

445. 99 ____

446. 91 ____

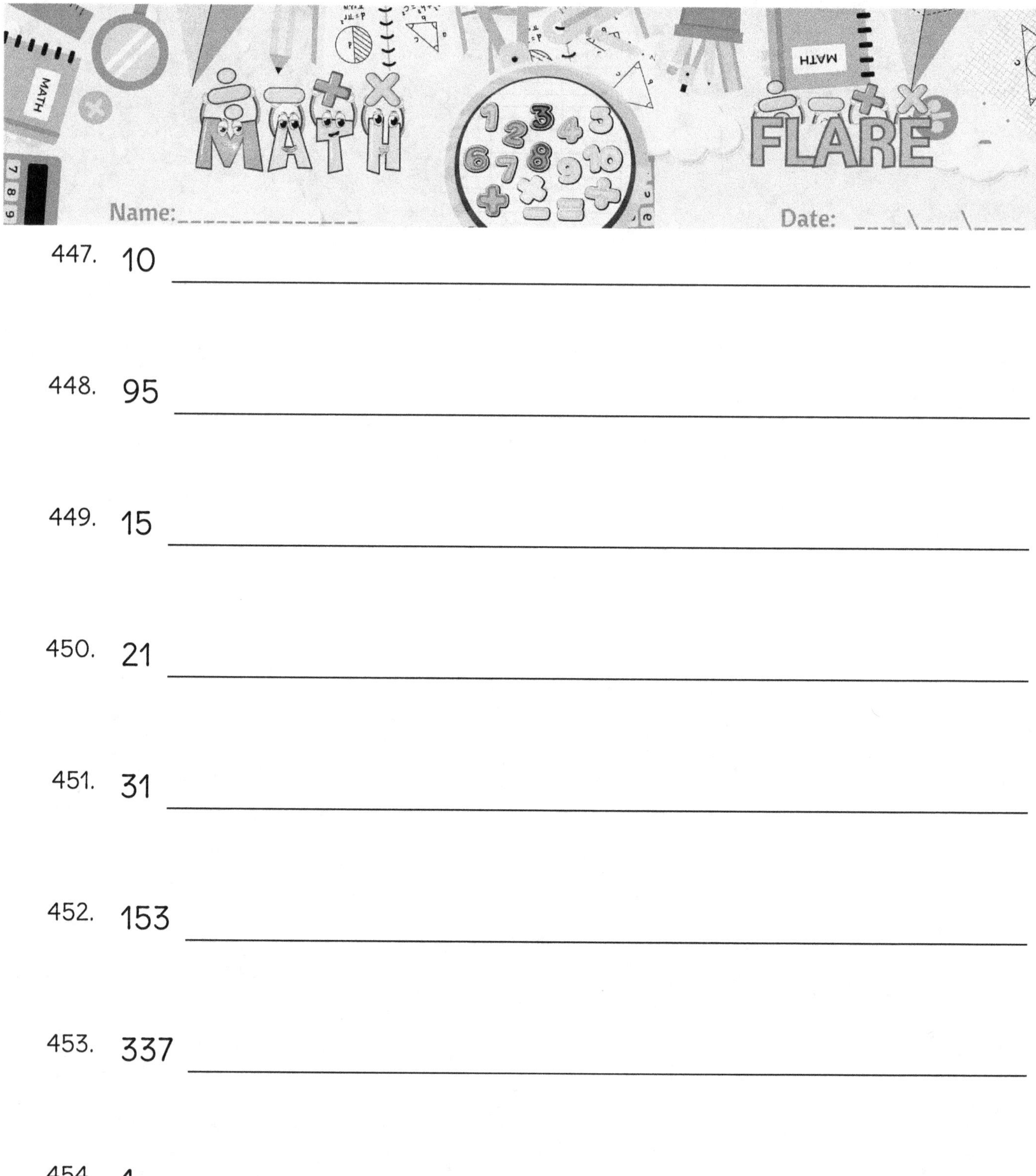

447. 10 __________________________

448. 95 __________________________

449. 15 __________________________

450. 21 __________________________

451. 31 __________________________

452. 153 __________________________

453. 337 __________________________

454. 4 __________________________

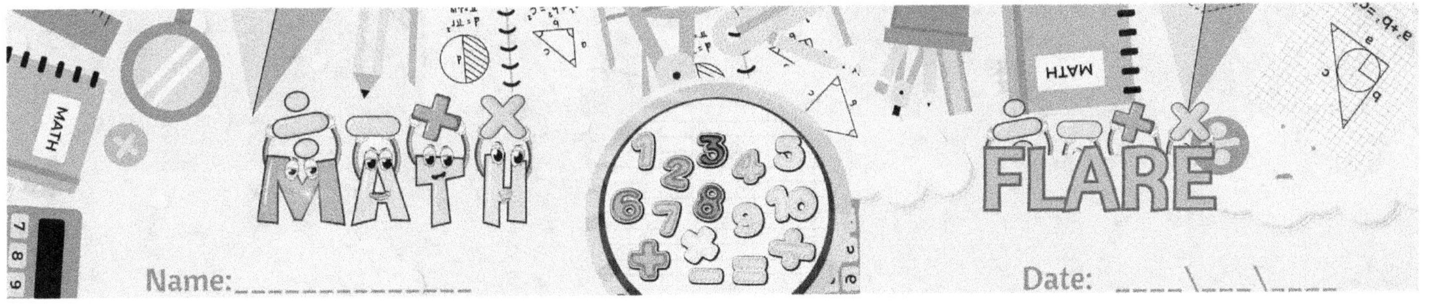

Prime Numbers
Is the number prime? List the prime factors for each number.

455. 37 = _______________

456. 7 = _______________

457. 329 = _______________

458. 490 = _______________

459. 370 = _______________

460. 91 = _______________

461. 88 = _______________

462. 223 = _______________

463. 197 = _______________

464. 78 = _______________

465. 5 = _______________

466. 9 = _______________

467. 29 = _______________

468. 297 = _______________

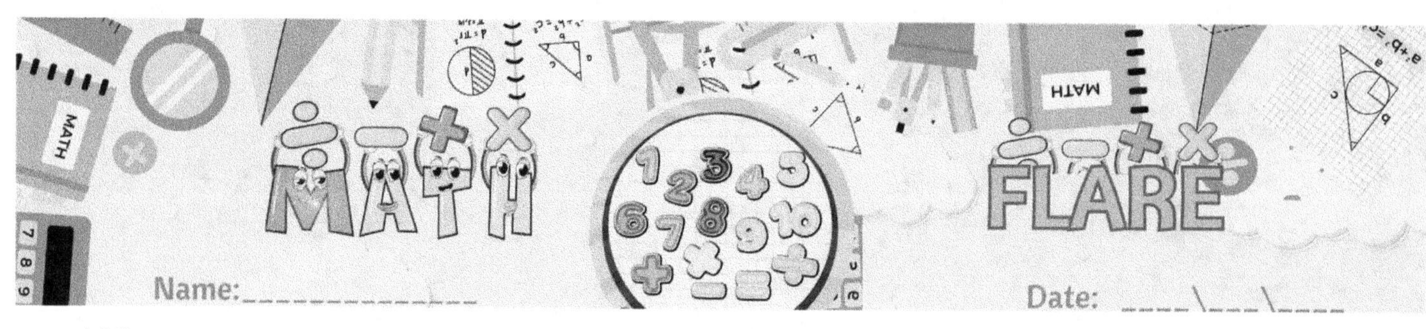

Name: _______________ Date: ___/___/___

469. 8 = _______________

470. 70 = _______________

471. 99 = _______________

472. 68 = _______________

473. 97 = _______________

474. 59 = _______________

475. 6 = _______________

476. 80 = _______________

477. 121 = _______________

478. 58 = _______________

479. 351 = _______________

480. 94 = _______________

481. 1 = _______________

482. 282 = _______________

483. 170 = _______________

484. 41 = _______________

Greatest Common Factor

Find the greatest common factor.

485. 286
     341 _______

486. 480
     30 _______

487. 255
     215 _______

488. 354
     120 _______

489. 105
     196 _______

490. 319
       33
       ____

491. 111
      447
       ____

492. 440
      176
       ____

493. 469
      315
       ____

494. 254
      462
       ____

495.   98
      385
       ____

496. 24
      466 ___________________________ ___

497. 422
      464 ___________________________ ___

498. 234
      183 ___________________________ ___

499. 357
      350 ___________________________ ___

500. 110
      187 ___________________________ ___

501. 42
      112 ___________________________ ___

502. 393
      420

503. 330
      348

504. 415
      10

505. 465
      5

506. 225
      255

507. 250
      85

508. 354
      398
      ___

509. 355
      375
      ___

510.   7
       91
      ___

511. 147
      363
      ___

512. 329
      210
      ___

513. 220
      198
      ___

514. 240
      192 ________________________________ ____

515. 348
      270 ________________________________ ____

516. 428
      130 ________________________________ ____

517. 114
      357 ________________________________ ____

518. 250
      185 ________________________________ ____

519. 258
       38 ________________________________ ____

Multiples

520. 359 _______________________________

521. 70 _______________________________

522. 37 _______________________________

523. 3 _______________________________

524. 83 _______________________________

525. 1 _______________________________

526. 11 _______________________________

527. 193 _______________________________

528. 8

529. 2

530. 9

531. 15

532. 86

533. 395

534. 103

535. 64

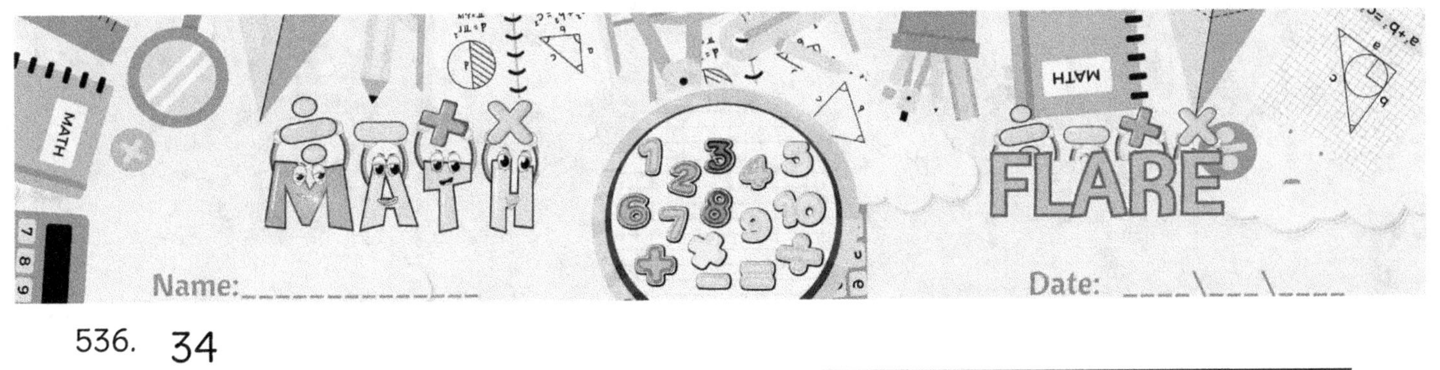

536. 34 ____

537. 117 ____

538. 378 ____

539. 33 ____

540. 68 ____

541. 320 ____

542. 63 ____

543. 5 ____

544. 373 _______________________________

545. 12 _______________________________

546. 6 _______________________________

547. 94 _______________________________

548. 20 _______________________________

549. 43 _______________________________

550. 38 _______________________________

551. 91 _______________________________

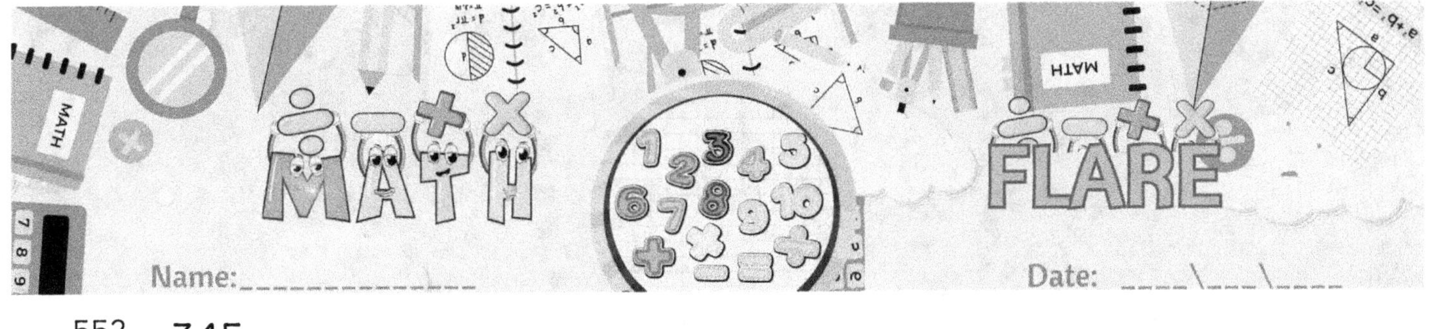

552. 345 ___________________________________

553. 209 ___________________________________

554. 183 ___________________________________

555. 102 ___________________________________

556. 4 ___________________________________

557. 27 ___________________________________

558. 229 ___________________________________

559. 66 ___________________________________

Lowest Common Multiple

Find the lowest common multiple.

560.   3
        8

561.   18
     483

562.   4
     179

563.   6
    12

564.   3
    25

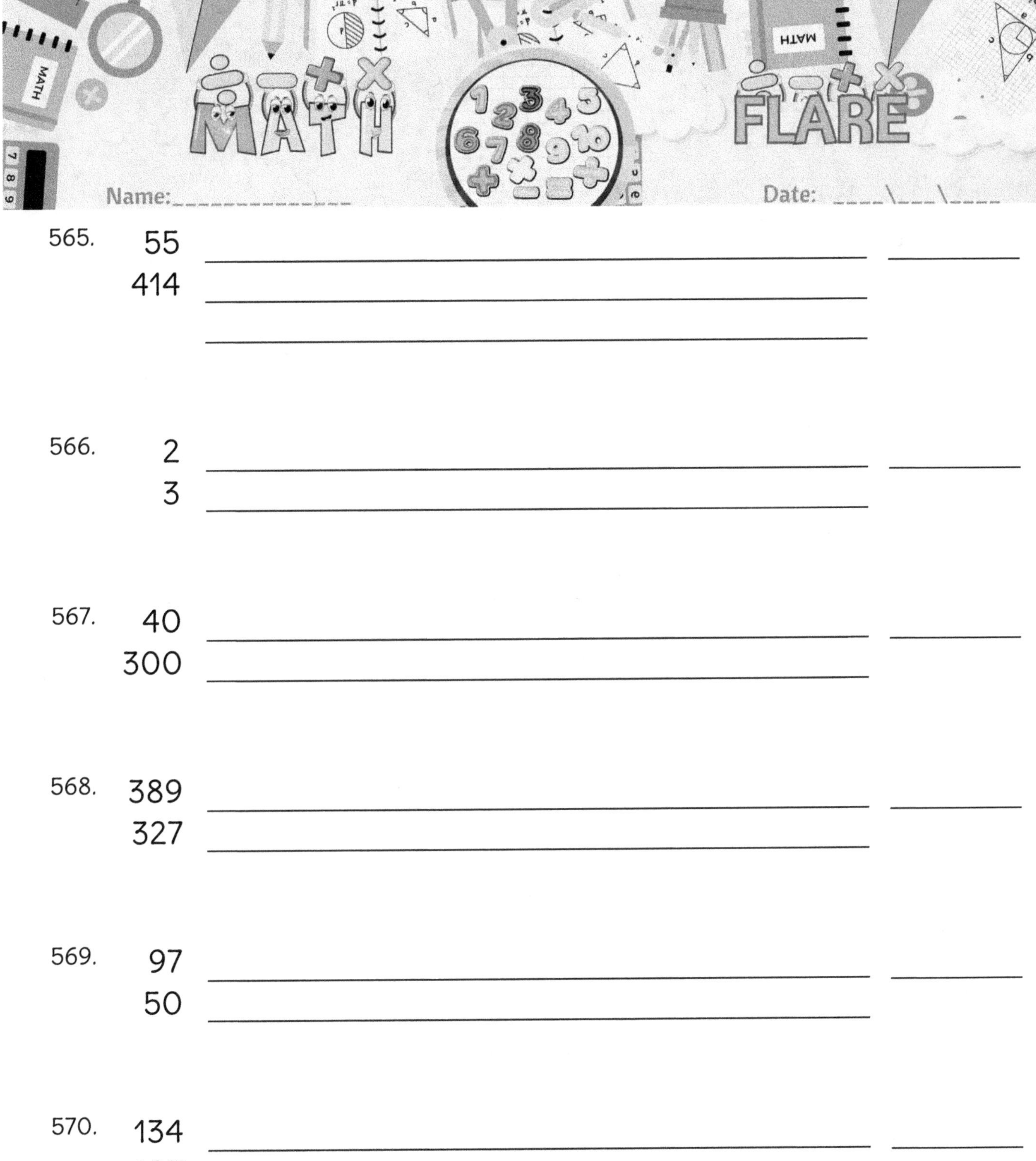

565. 55
414

566. 2
3

567. 40
300

568. 389
327

569. 97
50

570. 134
107

571. 8 _________________________________ __________
      4 _________________________________

572. 8 _________________________________ __________
      3 _________________________________

573. 263 _______________________________ __________
        6 _______________________________

574.   3 _______________________________ __________
       51 _______________________________

575. 337 _______________________________ __________

        8 _______________________________

576.   5 _______________________________ __________
       45 _______________________________

577. 148
       57

578. 455
       44

579. 487
        8

580.   8
       40

581. 233
        4

582.   95
       28

583. 445
      384

      _______________________________   ___________
      ____
      ____

584.   80
      127

      _______________________________   ___________
      ____

585.   99
       77

      _______________________________   ___________
      ____

586.   5
      239

      _______________________________   ___________
      ____

587.   30
       84

      _______________________________   ___________
      ____

588. 142
      219

      _______________________________   ___________
      ____

ANSWERS

Page 1: Whole Numbers and Operations

1. -6   2. -9   3. -20   4. 6   5. -2   6. -14   7. -13   8. -2

9. -7   10. 3   11. 5   12. 7   13. 4   14. 7   15. -6   16. 2

17. -19   18. 4   19. -5   20. -11   21. 6   22. -4   23. 7   24. 3

25. 3   26. -4   27. 0   28. -6   29. 4   30. -15   31. 1   32. -11

33. -1   34. 3   35. 0   36. -9   37. 6   38. -11   39. -5   40. 5

41. 6   42. -13   43. 7   44. 4   45. -11   46. -2   47. -9   48. -6

49. 12   50. 4

Page 6: Fraction Identification

51. 1/4   52. 9/10   53. 3/4   54. 2/5   55. 1/4   56. 11/12

57. 2/3   58. 1/2   59. 2/3   60. 6/7   61. 1/3   62. 7/9

63. 1/8   64. 1/15   65. 1/12   66. 15/16 67. 1/3   68. 5/6

69. 1/9   70. 4/7   71. 3/5   72. 1/2   73. 3/4   74. 11/16

75. 3/8   76. 14/15 77. 2/7   78. 7/10   79. 4/5   80. 3/7

Page 10: Compare the Fractions

81. <   82. <   83. <   84. >   85. <   86. <   87. >   88. >   89. <

90. <   91. >   92. <   93. <   94. <   95. >   96. >   97. <   98. <

99. >   100. <   101. <   102. >   103. >   104. <   105. <   106. <   107. >

108. <   109. >   110. >   111. <   112. >   113. >   114. >   115. <   116. >

Page 13: Equivalent Fractions

117. 96   118. 60   119. 24   120. 32   121. 2   122. 3   123. 9   124. 40

125. 16   126. 36   127. 20   128. 14   129. 12   130. 6   131. 95   132. 10

133. 15   134. 68   135. 30   136. 13   137. 36   138. 11   139. 5   140. 16

141. 3   142. 34   143. 9   144. 18   145. 57   146. 10   147. 8   148. 13

149. 30   150. 5

Page 16: Fractions Addition: Uncommon Denominator

151. 5/12   152. 8/21   153. 125/144   154. 2/3

155. 103/130   156. 23/33   157. 61/85   158. 21/55

159. 7/8   160. 37/40   161. 59/91   162. 43/44

163. 41/72   164. 2/3   165. 49/60   166. 9/28

167. 11/16   168. 19/78   169. 3/4   170. 74/99

171. 5/12   172. 31/42   173. 15/16   174. 67/182

175. 5/7   176. 5/6   177. 55/68   178. 271/304

179. 11/15   180. 31/36   181. 205/234   182. 13/18

183. 5/6   184. 13/20   185. 89/119   186. 25/33

187. 2/3   188. 249/260   189. 59/90   190. 62/63

Page 19: Fractions Subtraction - Uncommon Denominator

191. 19/204   192. 13/57   193. 15/17   194. 7/48

195. 8/65   196. 3/10   197. 7/15   198. 5/36

199. 1/4   200. 43/136   201. 1/5   202. 17/60

203. 1/12   204. 7/30   205. 63/220   206. 22/51

207. 105/209   208. 5/21   209. 7/16   210. 41/56

211. 19/60   212. 8/33   213. 1/12   214. 158/247

215. 5/12   216. 23/30   217. 29/63   218. 1/14

219. 34/55   220. 7/15   221. 7/18   222. 17/24

223. 19/30   224. 3/5   225. 3/8   226. 1/2

Page 22: Fractions Multiplication

227. 1/182   228. 4/25   229. 18/65   230. 22/105   231. 1/4

232. 2/63   233. 3/10   234. 3/88   235. 1/12   236. 7/50

237. 5/13   238. 3/55   239. 1/15   240. 13/32   241. 3/16

242. 1/4   243. 9/70   244. 2/9   245. 1/3   246. 3/8

247. 6/35   248. 9/22   249. 21/143   250. 3/5   251. 4/27

252. 11/21   253. 1/14   254. 5/39   255. 1/3   256. 5/24

257. 1/5   258. 1/7   259. 5/96   260. 7/12

Page 25: Fractions Division

261. 1 1/6   262. 16/25   263. 1/4   264. 7/9   265. 2 3/4

266. 1 1/5   267. 1/5   268. 35/48   269. 2/3   270. 2 7/10

271. 1 1/14   272. 7 1/3   273. 22/25   274. 6/11   275. 1/3

276. 1 1/2   277. 2/3   278. 1 1/3   279. 9/25   280. 3 1/3

281. 11/16   282. 9/22   283. 22/81   284. 1 1/14   285. 1 1/7

286. 1 1/5   287. 5/8   288. 1 1/2   289. 2 2/5   290. 7 1/7

291. 2/3 292. 7/8 293. 1 1/6 294. 2 14/33

Page 28: Mixed Numbers: Improper Fractions

295. 17/2 296. 137/17 297. 8 1/8 298. 3 11/12 299. 57/7

300. 37/24 301. 6 3/4 302. 93/17 303. 213/28 304. 71/18

305. 8 7/10 306. 79/9 307. 5 2/11 308. 5 3/16 309. 273/34

310. 43/32 311. 7 2/5 312. 15/2 313. 7 15/26 314. 9 1/4

315. 7 17/30 316. 6 1/2 317. 16/13 318. 41/9 319. 107/14

320. 4 5/34 321. 3 14/15 322. 5 3/19 323. 47/16 324. 5 7/10

325. 6 1/6 326. 45/16 327. 1 4/5 328. 8 2/9 329. 189/19

330. 33/4 331. 107/15 332. 3 1/2 333. 2 2/7 334. 7 3/11

Page 31: Exponents

335. 1,728 336. 160,000 337. 1 338. 1/5832

339. 50,625 340. 1/1000 341. 8,000 342. 83,521

343. 1/2197 344. 1 345. 1/196 346. 1/324

347. 64 348. 512 349. 625 350. 1/16

351. 169 352. 16 353. 1/1331 354. 1/6859

355. 64 356. 729 357. 289 358. 256

359. 1/121 360. 1/3375 361. 1/225 362. 1/361

363. 28,561 364. 1/144 365. 1 366. 1/27

367. 1/216 368. 1/36 369. 121 370. 1/4

371. 256 372. 1/25 373. 8 374. 81

Page 34: Square and Cube Roots

375. 1	376. 5	377. 5	378. 2	379. 8	380. 18	381. 6
382. 19	383. 2	384. 3	385. 42	386. 21	387. 22	388. 1
389. 9	390. 17	391. 18	392. 4	393. 12	394. 51	395. 3
396. 98	397. 15	398. 3	399. 8	400. 7	401. 10	402. 10
403. 8	404. 17	405. 23	406. 13	407. 24	408. 5	409. 13
410. 27	411. 20	412. 9	413. 6	414. 7		

Page 37: Factors

415. None

416. 2, 3, 6, 9

417. 5, 79

418. 2, 7, 14, 49

419. None

420. None

421. None

422. None

423. None

424. 2, 5, 7, 10, 14, 35

425. 2, 4

426. 3, 9, 43, 129

427. 2, 4, 8, 16, 29, 58, 116, 232

428. 2, 4, 19, 38

429. 3, 5, 15, 25

430. 2, 3, 4, 6, 8, 12

431. None

432. 3, 29

433. 5, 23

434. 5, 13

435. 2, 4, 17, 34

436. 2, 31

437. 2, 3

438. 3

439. 2, 3, 4, 5, 6, 8, 9, 10, 12, 15, 18, 20, 24, 30, 36, 40, 45, 60, 72, 90, 120, 180

440. 2, 3, 4, 6, 7, 8, 12, 14, 16, 21, 24, 28, 42, 48, 56, 84, 112, 168

441. None

442. 7

443. 2, 4, 8, 16, 32, 64

444. None

445. 3, 9, 11, 33

446. 7, 13

447. 2, 5

448. 5, 19

449. 3, 5

450. 3, 7

451. None

452. 3, 9, 17, 51

453. None

454. 2

Page 42:   Prime Numbers

455. 37 (Yes)

456. 7 (Yes)

457. 7×47 (No)

458. 2×5×7×7 (No)

459. 2×5×37 (No)

460. 7×13 (No)

461. 2×2×2×11 (No)

462. 223 (Yes)

463. 197 (Yes)

464. 2×3×13 (No)

465. 5 (Yes)

466. 3×3 (No)

467. 29 (Yes)

468. 3×3×3×11 (No)

469. 2×2×2 (No)

470. 2×5×7 (No)

471. 3×3×11 (No)

472. 2×2×17 (No)

473. 97 (Yes)

474. 59 (Yes)

475. 2×3 (No)

476. 2×2×2×2×5 (No)

477. 11×11 (No)

478. 2×29 (No)

479. 3×3×3×13 (No)

480. 2×47 (No)

481. 1 (No)

482. 2×3×47 (No)

483. 2×5×17 (No)

484. 41 (Yes)

Page 44:   Greatest Common Factor

485. 11
486. 30
487. 5
488. 6
489. 7
490. 11
491. 3

492. 88
493. 7
494. 2
495. 7
496. 2
497. 2
498. 3

499. 7
500. 11
501. 14
502. 3
503. 6
504. 5
505. 5

506. 15   507. 5   508. 2   509. 5   510. 7   511. 3   512. 7

513. 22   514. 48   515. 6   516. 2   517. 3   518. 5   519. 2

Page 50: Multiples

520. 359, 718, 1,077, 1,436, 1,795

521. 70, 140, 210, 280, 350

522. 37, 74, 111, 148, 185

523. 3, 6, 9, 12, 15

524. 83, 166, 249, 332, 415

525. 1, 2, 3, 4, 5

526. 11, 22, 33, 44, 55

527. 193, 386, 579, 772, 965

528. 8, 16, 24, 32, 40

529. 2, 4, 6, 8, 10

530. 9, 18, 27, 36, 45

531. 15, 30, 45, 60, 75

532. 86, 172, 258, 344, 430

533. 395, 790, 1,185, 1,580, 1,975

534. 103, 206, 309, 412, 515

535. 64, 128, 192, 256, 320

536. 34, 68, 102, 136, 170

537. 117, 234, 351, 468, 585

538. 378, 756, 1,134, 1,512, 1,890

539. 33, 66, 99, 132, 165

540. 68, 136, 204, 272, 340

541. 320, 640, 960, 1,280, 1,600

542. 63, 126, 189, 252, 315

543. 5, 10, 15, 20, 25

544. 373, 746, 1,119, 1,492, 1,865

545. 12, 24, 36, 48, 60

546. 6, 12, 18, 24, 30

547. 94, 188, 282, 376, 470

548. 20, 40, 60, 80, 100

549. 43, 86, 129, 172, 215

550. 38, 76, 114, 152, 190

551. 91, 182, 273, 364, 455

552. 345, 690, 1,035, 1,380, 1,725

553. 209, 418, 627, 836, 1,045

554. 183, 366, 549, 732, 915

555. 102, 204, 306, 408, 510

556. 4, 8, 12, 16, 20

557. 27, 54, 81, 108, 135

558. 229, 458, 687, 916, 1,145

559. 66, 132, 198, 264, 330

Page 55: Lowest Common Multiple

560. 24

561. 2,898

562. 716

563. 12

564. 75

565. 22,770

566. 6

567. 600

568. 127,203

569. 4,850

570. 14,338

571. 8

572. 24

573. 1,578

574. 51

575. 2,696

576. 45

577. 8,436

578. 20,020

579. 3,896

580. 40

581. 932

582. 2,660

583. 170,880

584. 10,160

585. 693

586. 1,195

587. 420

588. 31,098